M000112339

turn

north

at

divorce

10 Steps to an
Incredible New Life

Judy Kennedy, PhD
Julie Connolly, ACC

NOD, LLC

ISBN: 978-0-692-26992-3

Cover design by Bookfly Design

For you, the reader on your journey
to a new life.

— JK

To my clients who continually inspire
and educate me, and to my dear friend, Suzanne,
who embodies grace and resilience

— JC

To journey without being changed is to be a nomad. To change without journeying is to be a chameleon. To journey and be transformed by the journey is to be a pilgrim.

—MARK NEPO

We are pilgrims, you and I.

Contents

Preface

We are all on a similar path. We know our own heartbreak and pain of going through the process of divorce, and we can imagine what yours must be like.

Please know that this too shall end. You will be able to glimpse the sun peeking through the clouds. You will be able to see a new beginning coming to you even though it may seem impossible at times.

Divorce can feel like a public humiliation. You feel it when you try to give an explanation to friends or colleagues—you don't want to sound bitter, so you put on a brave face and say things like, "It's getting better," or "I am so much better off without him/her." All the while, you know it sounds a bit hollow. You look hard for the path through all this: the one where you don't have to qualify or explain things away, the one in which you feel whole and have your dignity. Know that you will find it.

You know in your heart you must transform your life. Some people talk about surviving divorce. What we want, and what we hope you want, is to not just survive but to create a beautiful and meaningful life.

The answer to survival isn't out there. It isn't in that new relationship you are waiting for. It isn't in that new location, new job, or new home. It's in you. There is a resting place in your heart and soul. There is a deep exhale waiting to happen. You can believe it. If you let this process of transformation touch you and teach you, you will relax, you will find your solid ground. You will feel safe. It is there waiting for you. All the while you have been worrying, looking, and it's been right there within you. Waiting.

INTRODUCTION

Three questions and ten steps to save your life.

....

There are no signposts in the sea.

—Vita Sackville-West

So it's happened, that catastrophic turning point. In the middle of your life of loving someone, you have become derailed. Everything takes on a surreal cast. This is the process of divorce, of separating from someone you love or once loved.

Most often true awakening happens in our greatest pain and distress. Divorce is one of these times. During this crisis we are offered the opportunity to really look at our inner worlds, recognize what is true and what is real, and point our compasses to true happiness.

You have been in uncharted waters before, though they may never have seemed as treacherous as these you are currently navigating. You may feel adrift with no sign of the shore and no idea how to find it. Where are the markers to guide you to safety? Should you yell for help? Should you paddle faster—but in which direction?

The search for solid ground following divorce can be lonely

and frightening. We have both been where you are, and with our training and life experience, we offer a compass to guide you back to solid ground.

But first you must float. Move with the current instead of fighting it. Let yourself drift; allow your curiosity to buoy you. Try to suspend your fear and anxiety. You don't need to be saved from these waters; you won't drown. You will be able to climb safely ashore when you are ready.

You won't return to the same shore that you left, but you will land firmly with purpose on another. Divorce is about re-orientation. The direction you thought you were headed has changed. Instead of fighting the headwinds, go with the flow. With an open mind-set, notice what is trying to present itself to you. What can you discover that will inform a new way of life? Who can you become? What will you be able to do when you land?

You'll discover three important aspects to turning your life around and coming out of this difficult time with a new life and a renewed sense of hope and joy. The following three questions and ten steps are the core of this book and provide a template to building a new life.

1. A New Lens: How Do I Create a New Story for Living an Authentic Life?

This book was written to help you not only change your focus, but to help you see your life and the world with different eyes. Shakespeare said it best: "Nothing is either bad nor good but thinking makes it so."

You must create a new story about who you are and how you operate in this world. This new lens or perspective about what has happened to you can dramatically advance your movement to a new life. It will attune you to yourself and help you identify your core values and act with integrity.

Changing the way you think or your mind-set is not easy, but it is crucial to this journey. Going through a divorce does not start with the divorce process. You have probably been unhappy and challenged for a long time. However you arrived at this moment, it happened either directly or indirectly because of your mind-set. Did you see yourself as a victim, as powerless? Did you think of yourself as someone helpful—your spouse was a project you were taking on?

This book is a guide to show you how you can shift your story from a negative or soul diminishing one to that of power and redemption.

2. What Resources Do I Have to Be the Best I Can Be?

The ten steps will give you all the resources you need to navigate the process to creating a wonderful new life. Each step offers practical tools to help you recover and move on. To change in a permanent way, you need to observe what is going on in you and around you, prepare for change, and cultivate tools that can change in your life.

3. How Do I Deeply and Profoundly Love Myself and Honor Who I Am as a Human Being?

You must start on the path of understanding your true and deepest nature if you are to navigate through and be transformed by your divorce. You are essentially and profoundly loved and lovable.

How to Use This Book

While this book is specific to divorce, the exercises and content are applicable to anyone who has recently come out of a committed relationship, finds him or herself alone, and wonders, *Now what?*

However, everyone reading this book will not be in the same place. That means some of the exercises and chapters may not be a good fit for you. We ask you to use this book as you see appropriate, depending on where you are in your own process. There are thought questions as well as exercises throughout the book at the end of each chapter. To deepen the content and let it take root, we strongly suggest you take time to think about these questions and then do the exercises. It is in quiet reflection that new options present themselves and seeds of a new life vision are sown.

Exercises

To fully learn and understand your own process as you navigate divorce or any life change and integrate what you are reading into it, it is important to express yourself. Expressing yourself in more than one way is even better. For instance, you are using your eyes to read content in the book. To further ingrain these ideas, write down what ideas resonate with you in a notebook or through a journaling app. You can draw or paint to capture your feelings. Perhaps you'll want to audibly record your thoughts and listen to them later. Using more than one sense to express yourself will add dimension and clarity to your process. As you approach the exercises at the end of each chapter, think about different ways in which you can express yourself.

Thought Questions

The thought questions invite you to pause and process the information before continuing to read. You may choose to journal or merely reflect. Depending on where you are in your transition, you may choose to go through the thought questions and leave the exercises until a later time when you have more energy. Either way, take the time to do some deep thinking. Based on our own experiences, years of helping others, and the most current research, we offer this guide as a resource to support you. But you remain your own best expert.

The value in the book is not from any wisdom that we impart. Rather, we ask you to consider the time spent on yourself as the value. You are spending disciplined time and creating the space to think about YOU and in so doing you are beginning to reclaim your life.

***

Judy's Story

Intimacy with oneself is not easily won.

My ex-husband and I were sitting in our lovely recently built home on the hurricane-prone east coast of Vero Beach, Florida. Our two beloved dogs, Namo and Bella, were glad to see us home, tails wagging, joyful that the pack was all together. We were sitting at our kitchen table, a favorite spot for talking about the day. It had been hard making the move to this house. Two hurricanes less than a month apart had welcomed us to Florida. We evacuated and were now home recovering from not having power or other essentials for three weeks. As if building a house was not enough turmoil, the hurricanes brought the realization that the world is impermanent.

I felt comfortable, so I wanted to talk about mundane things like what happened that day or whether we might have dinner at our favorite Thai restaurant. He was quiet, which was not unusual for him. He had wanted the move to Florida for career reasons; never in a million years would I have predicted that I would be living in Florida. I agreed to leave Seattle and commute back every month to see my clients. Living so far away was a risk, but I wanted our marriage to work and I wanted him to be happy

He turned to me and said out of the blue, "When are we going to stop this charade of a marriage?" I was totally unprepared for his callousness. The words took on a hurricane quality; I couldn't place them anywhere, they kept swirling around in my head.. As confused as I was, in some remote place in my being, I knew there was something missing.

Those 100-mile-an-hour words started me on a five-year quest to save our marriage. I am a couples therapist; the irony of my profession and my circumstances wasn't lost on me. Obviously I had not been paying attention. I knew that if we paid more attention to our marriage and saw the right person, we could save our marriage. We did see many therapists, some of the best. I was always eager to try something new. He was never in it.

As the truth became apparent—his emotional connection to other women, his lying, and other hard realities—I was confused by it all. It is all too painfully easy to slip into denial when what you want is not happening. That's where I was. I really didn't want to believe it. In a sense I colluded in our troubled dynamic by thinking that we could heal our marriage . I didn't understand that cheating, deception, and lying are character flaws and can't be fixed by working on the marriage.

I wanted to believe that "it takes two," so I went back into therapy myself. I constantly questioned myself and tried to be better.

We fell into the dynamic of deception on his part and vigilance on my part. I was seeking to find out the truth. Looking back, it is painful to me that the truth was like a neon sign in the room with me every day. He didn't want the marriage; he was untrue, and his immaturity wouldn't allow him to leave. I became resentful and terribly unhappy. I was actually numbing myself to those devastating words, moving as far away as I could from recognizing the truth: **We were done.**

Julie's Story

There is that moment when you know the person you married, who you still love, is no longer with you. You know before you actually know. Anything you find out after that moment is merely corroborative. They have left you while you were watching, and you are so alone. They didn't say goodbye in words; they just acted their way out the door.

It is in that moment of intuitive knowledge that part of you breaks. You continue down the path anyway with the partner you love, hoping things will turn out differently than how you know they will. And when your instincts are proven because the lies are uncovered, a part of you dies.

I remember having vivid dreams of walking around with hollowed eye sockets, wondering why no one noticed. You don't feel safe because you aren't. Your spouse doesn't have your back—they are no longer your family. It is scary and surreal and very dark. You begin to question if you ever really knew them.

I have been a self-motivated, achievement-oriented person from the time I was a child, always firmly believing that the power of my efforts would yield my desired outcome. This was a winning formula for a successful twenty-year corporate career, and so I applied it to my marriage. Imagine my surprised dismay when I discovered that it didn't work with a man who was emotionally unavailable. But I was tenacious. The worse his behavior became and the more he checked out, the harder I tried, redoubling my efforts, refusing to believe this was simply out of my control and that I was going to fail. I was so attached to my desired outcome of a happy marriage. Margaret Halsey once wrote, "The refusal to be defeated is a refusal to be educated." That was me.

We went to therapy together. I went to therapy alone. I read books. I left no stone unturned in my efforts to find the formula that would yield the happy ending I had pinned so many hopes upon. I became increasingly distanced from myself. I spent all my energy on coping and managing an impossible situation, leaving myself depleted and worn. The emotional loneliness in my marriage, fueled by feelings of betrayal, enveloped me in a swirling vortex of darkness and loss. In my grief and confusion, when my life was turned on its head, I looked for something to grasp. I sought traction. But there was nothing in the outer world that made sense. So I turned inward and, in so doing, returned home.

I reconnected with who I was, what I stood for, and who and what mattered to me. I relinquished control to my inner guides so they could lead me out of the abyss. Everyone has these inner guides—intuition and the core values that uniquely define who we are and how we need to live—but sometimes we drown them out in an effort to pursue what we think we want. Personal power lies in our ability to identify and listen to our inner guides. These guides will reveal new possibilities and pathways. Listening to mine provided me with direction and the peace I needed to heal. It is this sense of personal homecoming that I wish to share with you as you navigate your own transition.

Meeting Your True Self

Then it was as if I suddenly saw the secret beauty of their hearts, the depths of their hearts where neither sin nor desire nor self-knowledge can reach, the core of their reality, the person that each one is in the eyes of the Divine. If only they could all see themselves as they really are. If only we could see each other that way all the time. There would be no more war, no more hatred, no more cruelty, no more greed. ... I suppose the big problem would be that we would fall down and worship each other.

—THOMAS MERTON

Do you see yourself as you truly are, or do you think there is something basically wrong with you? Do you spend a great deal of time trying to compensate for these perceived deficiencies? Do you react too quickly to perceived threats, trying to cover up or be someone you are not?

As you navigate your divorce, it is essential that you ask yourself these profound questions: Who am I in this life, and how do I get in touch with my true nature, my basic goodness? As Thomas Merton says, we are in the "eyes of the Divine." If only we could see ourselves as we truly are, we would be freed from our doubts and feelings of unworthiness. You are essentially and profoundly loved and lovable. You must understand your true and divine nature if you are to navigate and be transformed through your divorce.

Personality is a combination of genetics and the patterns we develop over a lifetime to protect our psyches and navigate life. So the question becomes one of attuning. Who are you really? Surely you are not just your personality. Who are you, then, beyond those patterns and roles by which others identify you?

Who is witnessing these patterns? Who notices your thoughts and is paying attention?

How do we solve the question of "Who Am I"? This question leads us on a quest to discover and be attuned to the most essential core of our beings. As Shakespeare wrote, "To thine own self be true." This is harder than it sounds. So how do we honor this wise sentiment? First, check in with the self you are trying to be true to. Attunement is when your behaviors and emotions line up with your true goodness, your true and authentic self. It is a sense of self-congruency.

Attuning can involve slowing down, writing, meditating, becoming quiet, embracing silence, and noticing what you are experiencing rather than running on autopilot. Checking in tends to involve tuning in to our bodies or to our "higher selves," rather than tuning in to our "monkey minds" (the running commentary that we are telling ourselves).

A Story from Judy

Betty and Tom came in to see me as a very troubled couple. Tom was an executive who had strong opinions about everything, including what Betty should and should not be doing. Betty was a little overweight, much to Tom's dissatisfaction. At our first session when I asked Tom what was going on in his marriage, what was troubling him, he pointed at Betty and said, "Well, just look at her, she's disgusting." I noticed Betty's look of shock, but she didn't say anything.

Her shame was palpable.

Needless to say, both Tom and Betty had much to work to do both individually and as a couple. Tom needed to see his emotionally abusive ways and the fear that lay behind his hurtful behavior. Betty needed to work with and recognize her shame and feelings of unworthiness.

As Betty began to see her worth, she was able to see the destructive patterns in her marriage. She was able to see Tom's defensive patterns and emotional abuse as his work. His view did not define who she was. Betty eventually left the marriage and regained her inner, true self—not because she left, but because she became attuned to her own beautiful worthiness.

Betty did not need Tom's good view of her to feel good about herself or to have a happy life. She worked hard in therapy and in exploring her spiritual life. She was attuned with her own true nature.

Just like Betty, there is a desire within each of us, in the deep center of ourselves that we call our hearts. We were born with it; it is never completely satisfied; and it never dies. It is our true nature. We are often unaware of it, but it is always awake. It is the human desire for love. Every person on this earth yearns to love, be loved, and know love; sometimes like Betty we will give ourselves away by trying to please our partners or believing their view of us. Our true identities, our reasons for being, are to be found in this desire to be loved.

Going through divorce, we are tempted to shut down and close our hearts. In doing this we essentially cut ourselves off from our true nature and the truth that gives us the inner nourishment to live a happy life.

This transition in your life is the gateway to becoming more attuned to who you are and how you want to be in the world. Going through a divorce is a crucial juncture, a fork in the road, so to speak. So many people will harden their hearts, close off their inner being, and shun vulnerability in order not to risk the pain of losing again. Choosing love will open spaces of immense beauty and joy for you, but you will be hurt. It is part of the human package. You already know this. You have retreated from love countless times in your life because of it. We all have. We have been and will be hurt by the loss of loved ones, by what they have done to us and we to them, but you must stand up.

Being who you are in the truest sense is the way to navigate this difficult process to a happier and more fulfilled life. This is key. By choosing to keep your heart open, you will be transformed over time by the real meaning of love and become more in tune with your true nature, which is love itself.

Exercise: Your Love Story

Instead of trying to know what love is by abstract concepts and definitions, see if you can recall an experience of just being in love when love became radically freeing for you. For example, here is how some others have responded.

"I just sat there, absorbed by the beauty. It was not simply the sunset; it was everything and everyone. It felt as though I had fallen in love with everything."

Another person related love to romance:

"Sometimes when I was with him, things would just open up. I don't know how else to say it. I felt I was in love with the whole world, and it loved me."

Still another talked about worship:

"There are times when the routine of ritual falls away and I'm just there, and everyone is there, and the whole world is there, all one in love."

One spoke of childhood:

"I can't quite remember, but I know the feeling. Maybe I'd be playing in the sun or lying on my bed, and [I'd] just feel so warm, as if I were being held."

Some people cannot actually recall such experiences, but instead sense a kind of background knowledge, an awareness that something like this does exist somewhere, and always has. Whatever your experience, try to be honest with it.

Thought Questions

Recall some experiences of love for places or possessions. What did those experiences of love feel like? How did they affect you?

What is your experience of love right now? How do you sense yourself loving, being loved, being in love?

What are your desires for love: your hopes, dreams, and fantasies?

Exercise: Mindfulness Meditation, 15 minutes or longer (set a timer)

From the time we wake up to the time we go to sleep, we make important decisions on what we will pay attention to. Our inner lives expand or shrink in direct proportion to what we focus on. It's an existential choice; that is, we are responsible for how we spend our time. Mindfulness and mindfulness meditation is a conscious willingness to fully enter into life just as it is. Manjusrimitra, an ancient saint of Tibetan Buddhism, called it "pure and total presence." Thomas Kelly, a twentieth-century American Quaker, called it "continuously renewed immediacy." To create, to appreciate, and to truly love, we must wake up.

- Sit or lie in a comfortable position. You may choose to close your eyes or keep them open. If you are feeling tired it may be useful to let just a little bit of light in to keep you alert.

- Begin by gently moving your attention to the process of breathing. Simply observe each breath as it happens. Whether you focus on the rise and fall of your chest or abdomen or on the sensation of the breath at the nostrils, really feel what it is like to breathe. Don't try to alter your breath; just observe it as it happens.

- As you engage in this exercise, you may find that your mind wanders, caught by thoughts, noises in the room, or bodily sensations. When you notice this, know that this is OK; simply notice the distraction, but gently bring your attention back to the breath.

- Take a few moments to yourself, just to really feel connected with the present moment. Expand your awareness from the breath into the room around you. As you feel comfortable, open your eyes and bring the exercise to a close. Take a few moments to think about your experience and how you feel in the present moment.

Navigating Your Course:
Ten Steps to an Incredible New Life

Learn the alchemy true human beings know.
The moment you accept what troubles you've
been given, the door will open.

—RUMI

Step 1: Survive

Tools and Structures to Get Through the Hardest Part

....

My survival was up to me. I had nothing and I had no one. What I did have, I told myself, was my mind, my imagination, my memory, my feelings, my spirit. These were important and powerful things.

—JOHN MARSDEN

This may well be the hardest time of your life, unless you have suffered the death of a child. Most therapists agree that divorce is even worse than the death of a spouse. As hard as it is to lose a spouse to death, there are happy memories and other things to sustain you. With divorce, there is often the pain of betrayal and a huge blow to self-esteem, which piles on top of all the grief of losing the one you love.

The time right after the parting can be an emotionally brutal time. Where you had a sense of home with your partner, you are now adrift on a sea of emotions. Also, there were all those practical things of life that you shared as a couple. Now you face doing everything on your own. Many friends will try to help and offer all kinds of advice but no one can really understand unless they have been through this devastating process of divorce.

The first step to embarking on your new life is surviving the pain you experience from letting go of your loved one. As humans, we recoil from pain. The idea of suffering is abhorrent. It is an unnatural idea to embrace pain and so we engage in resistant behaviors. We will do anything to avoid experiencing hurt; however, resistance ultimately depletes our energy and prolongs our suffering.

In these early steps, we will refer to energy and resistance frequently, as harnessing your energy and being aware of healing versus resistant behaviors is essential to recovery. Here are behaviors that will help you heal as you move through your grief:

Accept Where You Are

It doesn't matter how you got here. You can't go back, and you don't yet see the path forward. This reality seems so simple, but it is really hard to accept. Acceptance means you aren't wishing you could go back to a happier time, and you aren't impatiently waiting to feel better and move into the future. You are sitting in the moment, in the now, in your pain, and accepting that this is where you are. In resisting the urge to avoid emotional pain at all cost, you will actually heal faster.

Resist the temptation to fall into the avoidance trap, which is filled with diversions—things to buy, people to date, busyness, and sensory-dulling substances. Regardless of how you may attempt to escape pain with avoidant behaviors, pain is a stealthy nemesis, and it will creep up on you. No one successfully avoids it forever.

So try to embrace the transition you are experiencing instead of fighting it. You will get to the other side of your suffering when you are ready. Pain is an incredible teacher. Instead of fighting it, partner with it to learn what you need to prepare for a wonderful future. You can be in pain and with pain without allowing it to be your host. As with any unwelcome guest, it will eventually leave. So be patient with yourself and use this time to learn.

The good news: this can be a hard road, and a long one, but you will come out of it feeling better, happier, and very much a survivor. Studies show that even when a person didn't initially want the divorce, seventy-five percent ultimately conclude that divorce was the right thing for them. We are programmed for survival. We are programmed to find contentment and happiness. It is our true nature.

Set Realistic Expectations

You will experience extreme emotional swings and lowered energy levels. Most likely, the holidays will prove challenging. You may have strained relationships with some of your couple friends or with your children. From time to time you may feel unhinged. It's OK. You aren't going to be the one person who can be a superhero and move seamlessly into your new singlehood. Give yourself a break. Don't expect so much of yourself during this time. Don't regard yourself with dismay if you find you are crying a lot or feeling rage and frustration. Refrain from telling yourself that it has been months, so you should get over it. If you have slept for ten hours and still feel exhausted, don't waste time wondering what is wrong with you. Nothing is.

Reject the idea that you should be feeling, acting, or thinking differently. On the other hand, don't plan on being in a perpetual state of hell so that when you do find yourself enjoying something, you experience guilt. Just because you're recently divorced doesn't mean you can't laugh, find someone attractive, or indulge in a vacation.

Instead of judging your divorce as the worst thing ever, try to greet your transition with equanimity, viewing it as neither bad nor good. This will leave you with some energy to begin to ponder: What lies on the other side? Who will I be?

Remember to Celebrate

To prevent internalizing the failure of your marriage as your personal failure, you need to conscientiously acknowledge things you are doing well each day. They can be seemingly small, such as paying a bill, fitting in an exercise class, or mowing the lawn, but no positive thing you do should go unnoticed. When looking at a seemingly endless to-do list, reject the temptation to focus only on the tasks that still need to be done. For each item you check off the list, pause and experience the sense of accomplishment. Acknowledge yourself each day. You are a good person. You are trying your best during a challenging time. Give yourself a break.

Create Structure

In the beginning, grief can feel like being on the bottom of a lake. You must feel these emotions, but you must also begin to create structure for yourself. It is well known that in crisis one must create routine and structure. Why? Because you are not thinking as you would in better times, structure gives you the practical safety of a routine and a feeling of normalcy when you are feeling emotionally homeless.

Plan what you will do during the day. Eat at the same time. Go to work as usual. If you don't have a job, look for something you can do that will feel satisfying and productive. It may be a good time to start volunteering. Go to bed at the same time every day. You may feel like a zombie doing these things, but eventually this structure will help you come out of your grief and back to a normal life.

A Story from Julie

I had a client who was depressed following her divorce. She was flat broke, looking for work, and getting very discouraged. When I first met her, she was hard-pressed to get out of bed. She described her time in bed as being in "Club Duvet." When she was better, she laughed that I was merciless about her leaving Club Duvet, but it was important for her to repair her self-image and feel like she had some control over her life. Together, we created a structure for her day that contained 10 elements. Yours will differ, both in number and content, but some of hers were:

- get out of bed
- go for a walk
- make the bed
- make a healthy meal

The point was to create some purpose in her day; these were tasks that she could expect to do. When she got through the list each day, she had a sense of accomplishment and control over her life.

We are not saying you should control every minute of your life. The structure serves the purpose of helping you get through one day to the next. As you do this, share your emotions with friends and, even better, with a coach or therapist. There are many support groups you can find. It also is very helpful to write about what you feel in a journal.

Manage Your Energy

What if your divorce is the conduit for discovering what you are meant to do and who you are meant to be? Following the breakup of your marriage, you have the opportunity to transform the energy that you focused on your relationship into a creative force that works for you and with you in visioning a new, fulfilling life. This creative energy is your true life partner.

But where do you find this energy? You may be feeling depressed and depleted. It may feel like you can barely put one foot in front of the other. How then can you possibly tap into the energy needed to create a new vision for your future? You actually have the energy, but you expend it in ways that aren't serving you—by feeling resistance, anxiety, and dread.

There are four areas to think about in managing your energy—physical, mental, emotional, and spiritual.

Physical. You may not believe you can take a walk when you feel so much pain; however, you must keep moving as best you can. Physical movement helps get your emotions back on track by promoting good things like oxytocin in your body. Oxytocin is the hormone secreted when mothers are nursing. It is a bonding hormone. When exercising, you produce the same hormone, and it makes you feel like being part of the human race again. Hug someone—your friends, your family, your children. The simple act of hugging produces oxytocin, which will in turn help you feel better and better.

Doing little things like watering the plants, going for a walk, or playing with the dog may seem small and of no consequence; however, things like these will help you eventually come out of a downward spiral and regain your footing in a new life. Even if you don't feel like it, doing small things will add to the energy of a good change. Don't think about it too much, just do these small things consistently and you will create a very positive upward momentum toward a new life.

Mental. Grief can lead to depression, but it doesn't have to. Going to work and being around others is invaluable. If you don't have a job, read about a new place or new activity that you have always wanted to go or do. Do crossword puzzles. Learn a new language. This will help you avoid mental fatigue. It is a common myth that when we feel mentally tired and overwhelmed we need rest. We don't need rest; we need nourishment to help us feel connected to life and not so alone.

Emotional. Long bouts of grief can make you feel emotionally drained. It is important to get your feelings out. Talk to your friends and especially your therapist or support group. In Step 7 we'll explore building our stories. We live by our narratives about ourselves, so be aware of the story you are telling yourself. Are you a victim? Will life be terrible and doomed from now on? Understand that what you believe about yourself and your life—the story you create about what has happened—also creates the emotions you feel.

Spiritual. What gives you meaning and purpose? Knowing this will sustain you through some very hard times of grief. If you have wanted to reconnect to your faith, this is the time to do it. If walks in nature nourish your soul, then make sure you do that. Reading about others' spiritual paths can also be inspiring. As the saying goes: What doesn't destroy us makes us stronger.

Commit to Self-Care

Sleep is hard to come by, particularly restful, deep sleep. With less sleep, you aren't energized and will feel more depressed, and eating habits often get worse. With less sleep, there is an increased craving for carbohydrates and sugar to boost serotonin levels in the brain. You may rationalize that you should treat yourself with junk food. Indulge yourself from time to time, but resist overeating or, on the other end, starving. Exercise even if it means putting off some chores. Program it in. Keep yourself up. Continue to take pride on how you present yourself, and pamper yourself when possible. If you can, get a massage, opt to read a good book, or soak in the tub. Regardless of what your treat may look like, program something in. You deserve it.

Set Boundaries with Your Ex

If you share custody of your children with your ex or have financial arrangements that bind you, you need to establish a new relationship dynamic. If you were in an abusive relationship, don't expect the manipulation or attempts to control you to end once the divorce decree is in place. Emotionally abusive people without professional help don't stop, so it is up to you to change the dynamic and script the message that there are new rules and limits in place. Going forward, regardless of your past relationship, you will not allow yourself to be disrespected and abused.

Set limits for communications that protect your space and emotional well-being. Discourage your ex from picking up the phone whenever he or she feels like it; set up a mutually convenient time to discuss business matters. Always put yourself first before agreeing to engage with them and do so only in a manner that will protect yourself. Unless you want to be friends, keep your discussions focused on relevant issues only.

If you want to maintain a friendship with your ex, respect his or her space following the divorce. Although you hate to see them hurt, you cannot own someone else's healing process and you don't want to create dependency. Allowing them to call you in needy moments will not accelerate the process for them; it will retard it. Space following a break up, even in the friendliest of splits, is healthy as each person claims responsibility for his or her own healing and recovery.

Create a Community of Support

Only through our connectedness to others can we really know and enhance the self. And only through working on the self can we begin to enhance our connectedness to others.

—Harriet Goldhor Lerner

As human beings, we need a tribe. We are relational beings, and to be at peak emotional fitness, we need connections with others. This is never more obvious than when losing your partner. Whether you initiated the divorce or they did, you will experience a loneliness you haven't experienced before. Unfortunately when you lose your marriage, friends often choose sides or are simply uncomfortable being around your divorce, so you lose some friends at the same time, compounding your feelings of isolation.

Having a support network greatly reduces the stress. Even if you go for days holed up in your apartment or house not talking with people, if you have a support network, you are not alone. You feel their presence even if you choose solitude over company. These are the people who will call and check in or send a cheery note or invite you to join their family on the holidays. Here are some of the benefits of having a support network along with the feelings these benefits bring:

- Sense of belonging: "I am not alone. I have a tribe."

- Validation: "I am OK. Other people love and accept me."

- Reality check: "I can only delude myself for so long before someone cries 'B.S.' and steers me back on course!"

- Security: "If I am sick or really depressed, I know who I can call."

What Does a Strong Community Look Like?

The support network may look very different from one person to the next. For some, it is primarily their family members. They enjoy unconditional love from their parents or siblings—people who truly know and value them. For some, it may be the family they choose: friends who have remained close throughout their life. And for some, their network may be comprised of coworkers, colleagues, and paid professionals with whom they have enjoyed conversation. A truly ideal network comprises all three groups, but few people have that ideal—so what is enough?

The strength of your network reflects the effort that you have expended in building it, and the priority to which you have, at this point in your life, assigned to it. It is not about being the most popular kid in school. If you don't have a lot of friends, it most likely is a function of your self-proclaimed independence, the effort you've devoted to making and keeping friends, or your reticence to share yourself. It is not because you are unlikable.

If you think you don't have many or any friends, it is not too late. You do need to make an effort, but the rewards are well worth it. A support system can be strong even if it is relatively new. You don't need friends you've known since sixth grade to have a meaningful network of support. You simply need people who recognize and appreciate your value and want to be there for you. So how do you build this if you don't have it?

Finding Your Tribe

If you have become isolated during your marriage for one reason or another, you might begin by reconnecting with friends with whom you used to be close. If you're in the same town, pick up the phone or send an email offering a few times to get together for lunch or coffee.

If you need to start from the ground up because you didn't make friends during your marriage or one of you moved away, consider activities where you might meet people who share your values.

- Volunteer: Every community has lots of options.

- Join a gym and participate in a class.

- Join a meetup group that you find online: They are in almost every city listed by area of interest.

- Start your own club that revolves around one of your interests: books, wine, gardening, cycling, etc.

- Take classes offered through adult continuing education programs.

- Join a support group.

- Join a professional or industry group.

Reading and paying attention to the news and other outside events will help you create a fresh perspective and feel more energized when you enter a new social situation. Avoid over-sharing your personal problems and practice effective listening skills so that you can pick up on things that may be interesting to the other person.

A Story from Julie

I have moved many times during my life, and I have tried every single one of the above ideas with success. As an only child who did not live close to either parent for most of my adult life, I had to. It takes energy, and it feels awkward at times—few of us love entering a room where we know no one. I can't tell you how many times I have done this and sometimes, I really dragged my feet. At times, it felt like a Herculean effort. But if you put on a smile, look approachable, ask questions of others, and keep consistently showing up, you soon figure out where you are most likely to find your tribe. Then you target your effort in that arena. Eventually, your efforts will pay off and you have friends who are there for you during tough times and who celebrate with you during happy times. Ideally you have this community before your marriage breaks down, but it's never too late to start the process.

What If I Am Too Overwhelmed to Look?

When you are in the throes or aftermath of your divorce, most people feel overwhelmed and depressed. The energy level required to build a support group is simply not there. It's all you can do to get out of bed and go to work. Furthermore, if you were the one dumped by your ex, you may feel like putting yourself out there could be exposing yourself to more rejection. You feel too vulnerable to extend a hand to anyone at the moment. If you are in this place, you need to do something, but it should require minimal discomfort and effort for maximum benefit.

There are three things even in this tired state you can try. First, join a divorce support group or get a therapist. You need a healthy outlet where you can process the difficult emotional swings you experience.

Second, exercise is crucial for both your physical and mental well-being. It is a healthy way to work out anger, decrease feelings of depression, and improve your self-image. If it is too expensive or your schedule won't allow you to join a class, buy a DVD or watch online videos that show a group exercising. Even this on-screen community will give you some sense of being with people.

Finally, if your schedule allows, volunteer. It may just be going once a week or bimonthly to the food pantry or grocery shopping for an elderly or disabled person. As Mark Twain said, "The best way to cheer yourself is to try to cheer someone else up."

Your Children Are Not Your Tribe

Your children cannot be your support system. Yes, you derive feelings of love and support by having them and being able to love them, but don't rely on them for your emotional well-being.

We've met people who have said that it was great to have their children, as they needed someone to love when their spouse left. One person described the kids as "filling [her] love tank." She was careful to follow up by saying that she didn't lean on them for emotional support, but just having them around to be objects of love was helpful.

31

You do need something to love. And if you have children, loving them is the normal course, but do be careful of putting all the energy you placed in your marriage onto them. They shouldn't be in a position where they feel responsible for you.

Don't Forget to Be a Good Friend

Your friends want to be there for you, but remember you need to be there for them too. They will also encounter challenges and bad days during your divorce. They may hesitate to bring things up with you, because you are the one who is perceived to have the bigger life event, so remember to ask. It is a two-way street, and eventually if you only call your friends to process your feelings, vent, or complain about your ex, you will wear out your welcome. They are sincere in wanting to support you, but don't expect it to be one-sided throughout your whole divorce. Try to consciously assess how you are contributing to the friendship. Send them a note every so often expressing your gratitude for their friendship. Take them out to their favorite coffee spot or restaurant.

Remember to differentiate between the role of therapist and friend. They aren't the same. Your therapist is paid to listen to you. Your friends are not. Always check in with your friend to see if it is a good time to talk and be clear about what you need. Do you need to vent or do you need a sounding board to help solve a particular problem? Don't call during their dinner hour, or when they have just gotten home from work. Frame it for them by asking if it would be OK to talk through something that is making you irate. This respects the boundaries of your relationship and lets them know they don't need to take care of you. You want their support, but you are able to take care of yourself.

Step 2: Grieve

Leaving or Left

We must embrace pain and burn it as fuel for our journey.

—KENJI MIYAZAWA

Grieving is an act of love. It begins when someone or something you love is lost. And grief is an essential part of transition. Rather than sapping one's energy, grief is part of the flow. It enables us to move forward because when we grieve, we are letting go of the past. You wouldn't feel grief if you weren't acknowledging the passing of someone or something.

A Story from Judy

In going through my own divorce, I was shocked at the amount of grief that seemed to come back over and over again. I have always been a self-confident person, and as a longtime meditator and spiritual person, I felt really grounded and peaceful. So when the divorce happened, I began to question myself and my ability to make good decisions.

Once on a Thursday I was feeling beaten down. You may have had this kind of day. All I could do was just fall into my bed and look up at the ceiling with my arm over my brow—it seemed dark even in the middle of the day. Why had this happened? I tried so hard to keep this from happening, but here it was nonetheless.

Strangely, I seemed to be on the bottom of a lake. The bottom was muddy, and the water was clouded. I could barely make out a faint light coming from the surface of the water and reaching down to me, stuck in the mud. I was alive but stuck, weighted down with my grief, unable to move. In fact I had no inclination to even want to move.

As hard as grief is, there is a certain calmness in it. It is a precursor to ultimately letting go. Even though I was in the deepest pain, I wanted to stay inside it, to be rocked by the deep current in the river and soothed by the flow of the water against my skin.

It's hard resisting the desire to just give up. You want to let yourself be there in grief and long for your old life. There is an odd comfort in not having to move, in just giving in to the overwhelming grief. Yet the faint light kept beckoning to me.

Suddenly I had an overwhelming feeling of grace and letting go. It flooded me with warmth and a profound peace. I surrendered to this reality and beauty. It was the grace that came out of letting go and surrendering, in the depths of my grief, to life--life with its ten thousand joys and ten thousand sorrows. I felt my heart open, making room for the pain, accepting the reality of my life and opening to the beauty of this life and love itself. I knew that I wanted to live my life from this moment on worthy of the grace that came to me in my darkest time.

The faint light coming from the surface of the water is waiting for you as it was for me. It is life, it is your life, and it is warm there. It is a beacon to you that life wants you even in your despair.

During my divorce process I learned in a very deep way what I have heard intellectually over the years in my Buddhist practice: Life is what it is. To have the expectation that it should be different is to suffer. To remember this lesson is to fall back onto the ground of being. We can't control what others do any more than we can control the sun or the moon. Believing that we are in control—if only we had done something different!—is to desperately cling to illusion. I feel deep gratitude for the opportunity that this loss gave to remember the old and true lessons. I am more at peace now. I feel more grounded in the deepest sense and I trust myself. I am not afraid.

What Are You Grieving?

Many have said, and it is true, that divorce is similar to experiencing death. But unlike death—wherein you are clearly grieving the departed person—in divorce, it isn't always clear what you're grieving. Yes, you are grieving for the person you loved, but also for yourself and the future you imagined you would have. Knowing what you are grieving is essential. You want to spend your grief energy letting go of the right thing. Anything that you don't let go takes up the space you need for the new.

Thought Questions

Consider the following common sources for grief in divorce. With which do you identify?

- **Your ex was a really good person and treated you well; you enjoyed his or her company. You were best friends. You miss this person for who they are. You ache without them in your life.**

- **Your ex was emotionally abusive or engaged in some behavior that disrespected you. But in the beginning, your partner put you on a pedestal. You are bitterly disappointed that your dreams for a happy marriage were crushed. There is so much lost hope to grieve.**

- **You feel completely lost. There was a structure that is gone. You don't feel a sense of self. You grieve your old identity, being part of a *we*. It feels like a big void with just *me*. You grieve the container that was your marriage. You grieve your role.**

- **You used to feel safe. You knew what to expect, even if it wasn't very good. There was a routine, predictability. You felt grounded. But now, the present and future are completely uncertain and you are afraid. You miss your old reality. You grieve comfort and a sense of security.**

This is by no means an exhaustive list of grief sources, but these are the most commonly experienced, and sometimes it is a combination of two or more. The key is to identify which are true for you, and then with this awareness, you can begin to process your grief.

Dr. Robert Neimeyer, a psychologist and professor at University of Memphis has written twenty-four books and over 300 articles on the subject of grief. He likens losing someone to having your book of life opened and all the chapters that follow today torn out. The central character is missing and you are in a position of having to rewrite the book. This presents both a formidable challenge and an incredible opportunity. How do you see it?

Dr. Neimeyer describes his process of healing from grief as "meaning reconstruction." By this he means we heal our grief through the retelling of our life stories, seeking to reaffirm and rebuild our lives in a world without a partner. We seek new meanings and a new audience to receive us after a loved one is gone. Who are we, and how is our world in light of our loss? The task of the rewrite, he asserts, will vary in difficulty depending upon an individual's culture, personal history, and personality. He invites people to consider how their loss shapes their sources of meaning. Neimeyer says, "I see grieving as a way of relearning the world in the wake of a loss."

Relearning the world is no small task and appears exhausting. And this is why, in part, grief triggers our resistance. Where to begin? All of a sudden, we are forced to consider huge questions, such as, "How can I create something that will matter to fill the empty pages?" or "What holds meaning for me now?" In what contexts can you operate or see yourself without your partner? The gift of being able to create new meaning for our lives, to author the empty pages, is not apparent until we are further along in the healing process and have a had chance to mourn. So be patient, but be hopeful. You will be able to create the starring role in your life.

Grief Versus Resistance

Grief suppressed becomes resistance. Grief expressed creates space for healing. The grieving process clears out the old to make way for the new. If we don't fully grieve what has died and let it shift us internally, we cannot create space for something new. If we don't allow ourselves to experience the pain and reflect upon the part we played, we will be more likely to repeat the old again and, not surprisingly, get the same result.

Resistance is defined as "any force tending to hinder motion." Whereas the grieving process enables forward movement and is expansive, resistance leaves us feeling stuck. There is grace in grief as we honor and respect our past by taking the time to say goodbye and reflect on the lessons learned.

That said, it is human to resist unwanted changes. This is especially true if we feel as though we don't have any control over what is happening to us. If you were left, you may literally feel like you might die. The unknown produces fear and anxiety. Our instinct is to pull back from things we fear and attempt to ward them off.

During bouts of resistance we tend to degrade ourselves. We may beg the ex to come back, promising anything as long as we can avoid this terrible pain—which is really fear. So if you are currently fighting the change in your life, practice self-compassion, but recognize what is happening and consider how embracing your transition may serve you better, enabling you to see the opportunity present instead of just the loss. Ask yourself if resistance is currently affecting your ability to move forward.

Envision the fighter in a closed stance: He protects his body and deflects what comes toward him. He is reactive and defensive. Alternatively, consider the martial arts principle that advises practitioners to accept the energy from the opponent and transform it through their bodies into personal power and strength.

How do you know if you are experiencing grief or resistance, since both have an overlapping effect of immobility?

Thought Questions

Listen to the questions you ask yourself and your inner dialogue. This is what resistance sounds and looks like.

- **"Why me? I can't believe this happened!"**

- **"Why did he/she do this to me? I don't deserve it!"**

- **Are you not dealing with the divorce, waiting until you get the second or third reminder from the attorney or your spouse that you need to sign something?**

- **Do you track your ex's activity to see if they have moved on with someone new?**

- **Are you holding on by re-reading cards or poring through photos?**

- **Are you feeling that in order to move forward you need closure in the form of one more conversation with your ex in an attempt get answers?**

These behaviors keep you hooked and only prolong the process.

A Story from Julie

I was guilty of resistance. Even though the divorce was my decision, it was still incredibly painful for me to let go of my attachment to the dream of a happy marriage. I looked at old photo albums and agonized over what had happened. It was inconceivable that the hope and love in our happy wedding pictures had become disillusion and despair. Had I tried hard enough? Could I step into a time machine and somehow go back to being the person I was once when the relationship was working for me? But there had been a shift. I had evolved, and the relationship had devolved. Finally, a friend wisely suggested I gather all my pictures and cards and put them in a box in a far corner in the attic and refrain from accessing them until I was stronger. It was then that I could move from resistance to grief and say a goodbye that honored our thirteen years.

Grieving: If You're the One Who Left

To varying degrees, the road to recovery after divorce (and your readiness to forgive) will depend on whether you were the one who left or the one who was left. And the distinction isn't always clear. You may have been emotionally abandoned and essentially dumped years before you actually decided to file divorce papers. You felt the rejection long before you experienced the guilt that goes along with leaving.

This said, when the decision to end the marriage is made—whether you are the person leaving or the one who was left—your story, what you tell yourself about your situation, determines your emotional path to recovery. This is because much of the recovery process depends upon the state of your self-image. If you are overwhelmed by feelings of rejection and failure, your healing process will take longer.

In making this choice, you have taken back the reins and become empowered. You are victim no more. You are being intentional instead of reactive. This is a completely different energy than feeling like the rug was pulled out from under you. As a result, you are further along in the grief cycle.

If you are the one leaving, most likely you already experienced the denial, much grieving, and even the bargaining stages of the grief process while you were still married. You have had time to come to terms with the decision and process a lot of pain. You have had the opportunity to study your financial situation and determine how you may adapt to more limited resources. You have reflected upon which friends you might lose and have taken steps to shore up your support network. You may have even begun to look ahead to the next phase in your life. When you are the decision maker, you may also feel less anger because you tend to feel less fear. You are in control of the situation instead of being surprised.

To be clear, regardless of whether you left or were left, no one escapes the grief cycle. It is only a matter of timing. Do you process it while you are still partnered and therefore your healing is faster following the actual divorce, or do you process it all during and after your divorce? The pain is there and no one escapes it.

Survivor's Guilt

A large part of the emotional burden on the one leaving is guilt. You own the decision and receive the fallout. While rejection and the accompanying hit to self-esteem that go along with it are brutal, the person who leaves often experiences a form of survivor's guilt. Unless you completely lack empathy, no one wants to hurt someone they used to love. Regardless of how broken down the relationship had become, your ex is a person for whom you deeply cared and to see them in pain and feel that you caused it can be agonizing. You may feel like you own his or her resulting misery.

If your ex was emotionally abusive and manipulative, they will project their pain onto you; don't expect them to own their bad behavior. And unbelievably, as the survivor, you may start to forget the lousy choices they made that caused you to leave your marriage. You may start to succumb to feelings of guilt or worse, self-doubt. You question whether you are making the right decision. Did you try hard enough? Did you exhaust absolutely every alternative? If you went to therapy, did you go often enough? Could it be with a different therapist you might be in a different place?

As a kind person who loved your ex, your instincts are to shield them from pain even if it is healthy for them to experience it. It is healthy not to want to inflict pain, but it is not healthy to protect your ex from experiencing the consequences from the choices they made. To attempt to protect them from themselves is a form of codependency. But feelings of guilt are powerful, and you may be tempted into "savior mode."

If You're Leaving a "Good Person"

If your ex didn't treat you badly, wasn't an addict, and didn't exhibit any bad behavior that people can easily identify as clear deal breakers, you may really be riddled with guilt. Who are you to leave a good person? This is really hard, but this is where you have to trust your intuition, your inner wisdom about what is best for you.

It is possible to simply grow apart. You've experienced this with friends before. Everyone changes and evolves throughout life. But we don't do it at the same pace, and sadly, sometimes two people who started out in a compatible place grow in very different directions.

Living authentically means living with intention and making choices that reflect who you are and what you value. There are times when you need to make difficult decisions, decisions that can cause pain to yourself and others. As an authentic person, you need to accept this. Choosing to end your marriage was a painful choice both for you and your spouse, but you were acting in integrity as soon as you concluded the relationship didn't serve or honor who you are. You won't always enjoy the consequences of your choices. You'll have second thoughts and moments of doubt when you question if you are doing the right thing. But in the end, to live authentically means not compromising what is dear to you in order to please someone else. You can't maintain a relationship that requires you to compromise who you are or limits your growth.

Grieving: If You're the One Who Is Left

Being left is a misnomer and can be misleading. It is often said that "it takes two" to make a marriage, and somehow this gives the person leaving justification for bad behavior. We all have issues in our relationships. The poet Rainer Maria Rilke said: "For one human being to love another; that is perhaps the most difficult of all our tasks, the ultimate, the last test and proof, the work for which all other work is but preparation."

It does take two to create a marriage and it takes two to keep the marriage going. Often the one who is left falls into the trap of shame, believing he or she could have done something differently. There are most likely many things that both partners could have done differently.

It is important to separate relationship issues and character issues.

Cheating, lying, and having affairs are character issues—not symptoms of you not being good enough or the marriage not working. These behaviors are not justification for a marriage that isn't working, and it is not your fault if your spouse decided to do these things.

Yes, you contributed to the marriage taking the form it did. No, you did not force your spouse into bad behavior. It is important to learn from your relationship issues, but not take on the shame of believing you were not good enough and deserved to be left.

It's Early for You

If you were left, understand that you are not as far in your grief as your spouse. You will be at the beginning of the grief cycle. He or she is already moving through and toward the end of that cycle. He or she is ready to move on and you are still in shock or depression. Treat yourself gently and give yourself time and space to work with your grief at this point.

If we go into a relationship expecting the other to fulfill us, it's doomed to fail. If both people go in with their self-love intact, then the relationship has more balance. It is a time of great learning when we can be who we are, and understand what love is and isn't.

There are lessons to learn. Give yourself time to reflect on what attracted you to this person: Often the people we attract in our lives are a reflection of where we are emotionally. If you have abandonment issues, you will most likely attract someone who will abandon you emotionally or physically.

If you were taught that love was when someone needs you, you will probably attract someone who is needy, and further, they are just a mirror for your own inner needy child that you have systematically abandoned.

Opening up our hearts to ourselves and loving ourselves unconditionally are essential steps in loving others in a balanced way

Divorce is very painful for both people, regardless of who left who. There's really no way around that. But in the end no one really remembers who left who. It doesn't really matter, does it? All that is significant is how you live your life from this point on.

Navigating the Process of Grief and Loss

Whether you are familiar with it or not, it is helpful to review the grief cycle as defined by Elizabeth Kubler-Ross. Being aware of these stages will help you come to release and resolution; however, grieving is an individual process, both in terms of duration and intensity. So we don't offer this model to suggest this is normative. We offer it because these are commonly experienced emotions and being aware of them, may help. Keep in mind this is not a linear process. You will oscillate from one stage to the next in an often-random order. Do not be surprised when you think you are done grieving and have accepted your loss that you come across a trigger that sends you reeling into grief all over again.

Shock. This is the body and mind's way of saving you from the devastating pain of the loss, at least initially. It is a blessing at best, but at worst can become a long-term numbness to feelings that resembles a living death. Usually it will pass naturally and in a short time.

Here's how shock may look in everyday life: You may wonder why you feel neutral when your life has been turned upside down. You walk around in a bit of a daze. You can't remember small things. You may continue to act as if life is going on as usual.

Denial. Denial protects us from becoming emotionally overwhelmed. Denial is a useful coping mechanism, as long as it doesn't keep you from progressing onto the next stage. After a while, refusing to face reality becomes a very unhelpful trait.

Here is an example of denial: You put off telling your friends what has happened. You continue to plan for the future as if nothing has happened. You don't really believe that he/she will actually go through with the divorce.

Anger. When you lose someone you love, it is natural to be angry for a period of time. You may be angry with the person for leaving you, angry with yourself for what you did or did not do to save the marriage, or angry with God for taking them away. You may just be angry at the unfairness and injustice of life. When your world is falling down around you, who better to blame for all your problems than an ex?

Bargaining. In this stage you will attempt to repair and undo the damage done to your life. Bargaining is when you stop and say, "Oh dear, I can't handle this emotionally. I'll negotiate anything with him/her, turn myself inside out if need be, but I can't go through this." It is an attempt to put on the brakes, stop that runaway train and get your life back. It might not have been a great life, but it was a lot better than what you are experiencing now. Bargaining is a last-ditch attempt to put off the decision to divorce.

Depression. Sadness, debilitating sadness, becomes your constant companion. This is the one stage we all expect. We know that depression is going to hit; what we don't realize is that depression can go hand in hand with all the stages of grief. For instance, during denial you may also not feel like bathing for three days or let yourself go in other ways. This is depression raising its head. Even the smallest activity, such as watering your plants, will go a long way to helping navigate depression.

Even though you may have surrounded yourself with a

good support system, when you're depressed is a good time to get some outside help. A good therapist or counselor can do wonders in helping you eliminate toxic emotions.

Acceptance. When it hits you, you will know it. The light becomes brighter. There is light at the end of the tunnel and life ahead. You've moved through adversity and learned from it. Full steam ahead! Even though you will start to feel better as you move forward into this stage in your life, even in acceptance you may still have negative emotions about your divorce. You may still feel some anger; there may still be sadness at the loss of your marriage. You may always have feelings of regret, but it is regret you can live with. You are no longer stuck in the mud in grief. If you're lucky, you are no longer grieving. If there are still feelings of grief, they are no longer holding you back from living life

Hold a Memorial Service

There is ritual to death that doesn't exist for life transitions such as divorce. Sometimes the formal act of saying goodbye allows us to lay a chapter to rest and move forward. You might try gathering all the artifacts of your relationship and saying goodbye to them in whatever manner feels true for you. If putting everything in a box and sealing it with tape feels like a burial, go for it. If burning everything in the fireplace feels better, do that. Maybe you want to write a letter that you may or may not mail. You can say goodbye in whatever manner you choose. Even if you intend to have a relationship or friendship with your ex in the future, say a clean goodbye to your old relationship. Allow the tears to flow. You've deserved it.

Exercise

1.　Write down everything you are grieving. Take a look at what you wrote and divide it into columns with these labels.

- •my ex
- •my dreams
- •my old self
- •my old life

These are the hooks that are keeping you attached to the past.

2.　For each item on the list, consider the cost of hanging on. Ask, "What will it take for me to let go?" Also write down what you see as possible for yourself if you let go. At this point, you may only be able to recognize the cost without yet seeing the possibilities, and that's fine. You can revisit this piece later after you are further along in your transition.

3.　Think about a memorial that will help you lay your past relationship to rest. What might honor the years you spent together? What can you do to create a sense of closure?

4.　Retell your life story: What can you start to create in order fill the empty pages? Think deeply about what matters to you. How can you begin to find meaning and define yourself? Write down how your loss is shaping your source of meaning in the world. What are some things you can do to step into the vacated role of central character in your book of life?

Step 3:
Let Go

Change Versus Transition

We are all faced with a series of great opportunities brilliantly disguised as impossible situations.
—Charles R. Swindoll

Change is purely a situational shift such as moving, switching jobs, or divorce. Change itself contains no inner life. One day, you are in job A and the next week you are in job B. You are married and then you are divorced. If we perceive the job change, the move, or the end of the marriage as the whole story, we cannot experience personal evolution.

But our temptation is to purely focus on the change. Change invites problem solving, which suggests a solution. Solutions are comfortable. This is where the physical divorce process resides as you and your attorney decide how to divide assets. Solutions are solid, finite, and require very little emotional energy. We solve problems of varying degrees of difficulty every day. We know how to do this. And we get a short-lived sense of accomplishment having done so.

An understanding of the real and important difference between change and transition is critical. In his book, *The Way of Transition*, William Bridges describes the three phases of transition as:

ending
neutral zone
beginning

The ending is just what it suggests—the death of something—followed by the neutral zone, also known as being in limbo. This is the most chaotic and nerve-racking phase because you have no direction and there is no time limit as to how long it will last. You have let go of your old reality without a clue as to what your new life looks like. It makes sense why you would do everything you could to resist this, right? (More on this later in the chapter.)

In embracing the uncertainty of this stage and being open to whatever is presented to us, our reward is moving into the final stage of transition, which is transformation. This stage is what differentiates transition from mere change: personal evolution. It invites us to look with a new lens at our current situation and seek the inherent opportunity. Instead of angrily resisting the change we face, we accept that the old reality is gone and that we need to redefine our relationship to the situation. Instead of reacting, we choose how to respond, asking, "What wants to happen?"

Note: This is a different question than "What do I want to make happen?" You are not looking to control the situation; you are looking to see what naturally presents itself as the gift. It is also important to ask: "What relationships, fears, attachments, or beliefs do I need to let go of in order to grow?"

Without asking these questions and being open to modifying our behavior and beliefs, we may experience physical change but not transition.

This is why divorce is so scary. But this process is the way to personal growth, and so embracing it, being open and curious about it requires courage and strength—and a leap of faith!

A Story From Julie

When my former husband and I moved from Seattle to Connecticut, the geographical shift was just the tip of the iceberg. In addition to saying goodbye to old friends and the house we built, I had to say goodbye to my old life and my relationship to it. I had spent twenty years in a successful and financially rewarding career as a CPA, progressively moving up into new leadership roles. But my career was no longer serving me. The feelings of restlessness and dissatisfaction that I had attempted to tamp down for years came to the surface as we prepared to move. I began to examine the beliefs I had attached to my career and my identity as a successful businesswoman. If I gave this up, how would I be financially secure again? More importantly, who would I be? What was the point of all the hard work?

The physical move across country forced me into the first stage of transition—saying goodbye. By the time we reached the opposite coast, I was in limbo. I felt lost without specific goals for the first time in my life and without any vestiges of familiarity. It was after floating for a little over a year and being open to following a winding road that I finally became aware of who I was and what I was meant to do. Filled with new purpose and armed with a vision, I signed up for a program to become a certified coach and landed a corporate contract and a couple of wonderful business partners to work with. It was all unknown and unplanned as recently as a couple years before.

Exercise

1.   Where are you in the 3 phases of transition? What emotions are you experiencing in this phase? Write down the physical changes that have happened.

2.   Write your story of divorce as a change. What problems have you solved? What do you need to solve?

3.   Now rewrite your divorce as a transition. What opportunity is possible? What new relationship with yourself is possible? What beliefs about yourself may be preventing you from letting go? Ask yourself, "What is the opportunity here?"

4.   If you are having difficulty seeing opportunity, consider the story of your struggle. What beliefs or fears are present?

5.   List another transition that happened in your life. What did you learn? What was the gift?

The Trapeze Artist

Everything you want is on the other side of fear.
—JACK CANFIELD

Often we think of change and transformation as an ending and then a new beginning. But it's more complicated than that. As you go through one of the hardest parts of change, the limbo stage, picture yourself as a trapeze artist: this is you as you go through this difficult transition. You swing out on the trapeze bar building momentum. You realize you need to change. The bar you are holding onto for dear life is your old life. It doesn't work any more, and you know you have to let go. You swing back and forth knowing you need to let go but so afraid of this crucial step. Who or what will catch me if I fall? I'm not even sure where I'm going. I feel so alone up here suspended all by myself!

Another reason that its hard to let go of the bar is that spending time in the neutral zone reminds of past wounds and traumas. There is a resonance between present painful circumstances and those that happened in the past.

This is the time to get on the other side of your fear. You feel the fear but you do not let it define you. This time teaches you what you need to know about finding the beauty that is in you. It is about finding that strength that you never realized you had. It holds the key to everything you need to know about waking up to your own strength.

This time is like a seed when it is underground, waiting to germinate, there doesn't seem to be much going on, but it's a very fertile and important time. You are in the process of shedding one identity and yet haven't fully taken on a new one. This is where the questioning, growth, learning, formation, courage, creativity, and risk-taking happens.

Our natural reaction is to fight for our rights and hold on to what we believe is ours. But until we surrender, we are glued to the pain of our breakup. Surrendering is especially difficult if we've been betrayed, abandoned, or deceived. But if we accept that everything is happening exactly as it should, we can begin to surrender and trust in the natural flow of life. To transcend our suffering, we must go against our instinct to hold on to the bar and instead have faith in our capacity as a human being. We can let go and reach for our new lives.

A Story from Judy

Beth, a young woman in her mid-thirties, was going through her second divorce. She always seemed to pick men who were not emotionally mature. Beth was abandoned by her father as a young child and never saw him again. She felt especially vulnerable at the ending of this second marriage and found it unusually hard to let go of perceived old comforts and ways of thinking, out of fear that her old feelings of abandonment would overwhelm her.

She had a very hard time being willing to open the floodgates of her grief. She was afraid that she wouldn't survive those deep, deep emotions of pain and loss. She was stuck in the neutral zone.

She began to eat more, stuffing the feelings down. She stayed in most of the time. She cut herself off from friends and family. Finally when she began to have overwhelming feelings of depression and anxiety, she sought help in therapy.

We worked together to create a safe place to allow the hard feelings to rise. She was courageous as she faced her emotions and fear of not being lovable. It was not an easy journey, but she was able to transform her old fearful mental model of who she was—an anxious, abandoned victim—to a wonderful, lovable person full of excitement for a new life. When those old feelings rear their head, she has the tools to deal with them. In this new state of being, she was able to attract a loving man and new friends in her life.

Letting go of our old lives, letting go of our anger and resentment, is a process. It doesn't happen in a linear way. You may feel as though you are through your ending only for the feelings to come back around again. This process involves letting go again and again. Don't become discouraged. For some people it happens in the first year; for others it takes longer.

Thought Questions

Here are some activities and ways of thinking that are helpful during this limbo time.

- **Expect that you will be experiencing the gamut of emotions from anger, to despair, to hopefulness and back to fear. This is normal. *You have emotions; you are not emotions.***

- **Be willing to question what you really want in life. It is a good time to be creative, but not necessarily a good time to make decisions. Try on different ways of thinking and new lifestyles. Don't limit yourself.**

- **Set some short-term goals for yourself. It's not the time to expect that you will lose fifty pounds, but committing to taking a walk everyday is achievable.**

- **Shift your attitude by understanding that this is a time for redefining yourself and reorienting your life. It is not a time of meaningless waiting. You may feel you are stuck and will never move out of this stage, but you will.**

- **Journal, paint, or go on a retreat. Take time to reflect about you and your life.**

- **Check in with a therapist or coach, if possible.**

Step 4:
Get Unstuck

Identify What Is Holding You Back

Growth is painful. Change is painful. But nothing is as painful as staying stuck somewhere you don't belong.
—MANDY HALE

Your divorce may have been over for a while, yet you don't feel like you're able to move on. Feeling stuck is miserable. You want to move forward because you know you would feel better if you did, but you can't. You don't know why.

That final step in the grieving process—acceptance—can remain elusive for a long time. We have spoken with people who report feeling devastated and staying in that state for years after the divorce. Why is this, and what can you do to avoid it?

Getting clear on why you aren't gaining traction and are stuck in the mud is actually the first step to getting out of it. If you are feeling stuck, consider that you may be experiencing resistance to change, especially if you weren't the one who wanted it. Specifically, you may be resisting letting go, fighting acceptance. This resistance takes the form of thoughts and questions that seek to undo the present. These thoughts and questions consume a lot of energy, and they conspire to keep you hooked into the past.

When people feel stuck they may wonder: Am I stuck or am I in limbo? As we discussed in the previous step, being in limbo is actually moving forward in your transition process, though as you swing between the past and a yet-unknown future, you may not feel like you're moving forward.

Being stuck is different. Being stuck looks like hanging on and refusing to let go. You're not swinging; you're just clinging.

Consider the following common scenarios that keep people hooked. See if any resonate with you. Once you identify them, you can use that awareness to start making changes in your behavior and move forward.

You Must See Your Ex Frequently

You may have to see him or her if you have children or live in the same town. Each encounter may invite you to wonder if things would be different if you were to reconcile. If your ex has a new relationship, seeing them may be particularly painful. Any sign of their happiness may seem a direct indictment against your ability to be a good partner. Your replacement must be smarter, cuter, younger—in short, better. Your ex's presence can become a constant reminder of your failed marriage and your perceived inadequacies. **You are stuck in requiring external validation that you are good, attractive, and loveable.**

Justice Has Not Been Served

Your ex may have cheated on you, lied to you, or otherwise abused you, and you want revenge. You at least want them to display the requisite amount of empathy and sorrow that you feel the situation (and your broken heart) deserve. You find it unbearable that they have seemingly glossed over all your pain and moved seamlessly, if not joyfully, forward with their life. When will Karma kick in? **You are stuck in anger and a desire for retribution.**

You Are Still Asking "Why?"

If you were betrayed, rejected, or abused, you may be stuck on asking why. You wonder if there is a reason that could be readily understood and maybe even accepted, if you just knew it. How could everything turn out so badly? Was it something you did or should have known? You repeat scenes of your marriage over and over—what you did, what your ex did—and you just can't understand what happened. **You are stuck in your need to understand—some call this "closure."**

One of You Made a Choice

When someone you are close to dies, it is out of your control. Divorce involves a decision either by you, your partner, or both of you. The fact that someone owns this choice can delay the process of moving on. If you were the one to choose to end the marriage, you bear the responsibility. You may be agonizing over whether this really is the best thing for you or your children. Have you exhausted all possibilities in trying to resuscitate the relationship? Have you given your ex enough chances to change? **You are stuck in survivor's guilt.**

If your partner made the decision, you feel completely out of control. How can someone you loved decide to throw you overboard? There must be something you can do to change their mind. There must be an implicit action step that will make the outcome different. **You are stuck feeling out of control and abandoned.**

Your Relationship Story

There are people who are known while they are alive as "that son of a bitch." Miraculously, once they die, they are canonized. Misdeeds aren't mentioned, and any attribute is extolled. Every good memory is repeated to anyone who will listen.

Relationships suffer the same rewrite once they end. Your relationship may have been filled with anxiety and characterized by tension, but once it is over, the loving times you held hands and the meaningful moments you shared become the whole story. The loneliness and struggle you are currently experiencing are contrasted to the cozy nights you snuggled by the fire, and you forget the sense of abandonment you felt when your ex checked out.

On the other hand, you may be fanning the flames of anger and resentment by focusing on the bad behavior that peppered your marriage. The whole of your partner is negated, and everything your ex ever did or thought was wrong or bad. For the marriage to have failed, they had to have been a rat—still are and always will be. The question still haunts you: How you could have entangled yourself with such a lowlife? You lament the wasted years. **You are stuck in your narrative.**

Attachment to the Outcome

You had a lot vested in the success of your union. You had dreams of a happy life with a wonderful partner. It didn't work out the way you hoped and part of you can't believe it. It is devastating to let go of your dream, partly because you are letting go of a piece of your identity at the same time. Who are you now? What are your beliefs about being part of a partnership? What values do you attach to being divorced? Is it OK that you tried your best and still have a failed marriage? Consciously or subconsciously, you are making comparisons between your current state and the dream of a partnered status and coming up short. **You are stuck in disappointment and lack of identity.**

Family of Origin Messages

Were you brought up to see things through to the end? Does being a committed person mean enduring with stoicism? Do your cultural and family beliefs inform your thinking that divorce is wrong? You probably know someone who was unhappy in his or her marriage and suffered through it, keeping the family intact until the kids were out of the house, or maybe they never left. Were they extolled as a role model either implicitly or explicitly? There are many subtle and not-so-subtle messages that seep into people's brains as they grow up. It is very difficult to contradict these messages. Guilt and feelings of failure and shame can take over—especially if you are the only member of your nuclear family to be divorced. You've seen friends and family members put up with mediocre marriages, what gives you the right to ask for more? **You are stuck in family or cultural guilt.**

Missing Structure

Humans are inherently relational, so connections with family, close friends, and a life partner are important to us. As part of a couple, you knew your role. You had part—or maybe all—of your identity entwined as part of an *us* and *we*. You enjoyed the stability that the structure of the relationship provided. It was who you presented to the outside world. Without it, you are adrift and alone—something that humans innately resist. If you are not part of a *we*, who are you? If this seemingly stable structure can fall apart, what can you count on? **You are stuck in loneliness and feelings of insecurity.**

You Still Love Your Partner

It is just so hard to let go. Whether your choice or your spouse's, it is scary to move on. Everything familiar is now estranged. When you have a victory or a disappointment, when you see something funny, your reflex is to reach out to your ex. After all, this was the person who knew you best. When you let them go, who will take their place? Can you let go of the past when you have nothing to turn to in the present? **You are stuck in love.**

Thought Questions

Find a quiet place and write down your responses to these questions.

Have you taken responsibility for your circumstances?
Too many people have a habit of blaming their circumstances or mistakes on bad fate, bad luck, or other people. Too few will admit that their situation is a direct outcome of the choices they've made. This is the foundation you need to correct in order to grow. You must accept your current situation, take responsibility for it, learn from it, make the necessary changes, and move forward.

Have you given in to being stuck?

Are you secretly enjoying just a little wallowing in your own grief and disappointment? This is allowing your fears to get the best of you. I'm not worthy and I'm not lovable are core fears. You are not helping yourself by allowing yourself to give in to these fears, and indulging in a pity party risks alienating your support group.

Have you really gotten in touch with your own calling, those things that make you feel alive?

Are you trying to satisfy other people in your life and not living your own life? You have to find something to believe in, something that anchors you and keeps you looking forward—regardless of what others are doing or saying. It is better to live your own destiny imperfectly than to live an imitation of somebody else's life with perfection.

Have you become accustomed to negativity and your attitude shows it?

It's not what you look at that matters, it's what you see. The biggest wall you must climb is the one you have built in your mind. If you don't control your attitude, it will control you. Avoid negative people, places, things, and habits. Don't give up.

Are you practicing gratitude?

Do you appreciate what you have? Pause for a moment. Breathe in slowly and deeply. Exhale. Feel the miracle of your breath. And say, "Thank you." You probably woke up with a few aches and pains this morning, but you woke up. You've seen better days, but you've also seen worse. You might not have everything you want right now, but you have everything you need to move forward. Life isn't perfect, but it is good. Visit gratefulness.org.

Do you still want your old life back?
You keep worrying about a time that no longer exists. You can't have a better today if you're still thinking and worrying about yesterday. Whatever could have been or should have been doesn't matter. This moment is here and now for you to live.

Do you keep looking for happiness outside yourself?
True happiness has nothing to do with material possessions; it is the surrender to an abundance that has no limit. What you seek is not somewhere else at some other time; what you seek is here and now, within you. The more you look for it outside yourself, the more it hides from you.

Step 5: Own Your Personal Power

Take Back What You Gave Away

Never allow someone to be your priority while allowing yourself to be their option.

—Mark Twain

In Larry Ackerman's book *The Identity Code*, he describes special relationships as ones "that become places of refuge, that protect and nurture the most sacred and beautiful aspect of your being ...you can recharge your engine with people who know what matters to you and who want what you have to give."

This is the type of marriage we imagine and hope we will have with our life partners; we want to feel that what matters most to us is also cherished by our spouses and that our relationships honor who we are and what we have to contribute.

But for each of us who have experienced divorce, our disappointment that this isn't the case is heartbreaking. And sometimes disappointment translates into self-doubt, so we question ourselves.

- Do I have anything valuable to offer?
- If my partner didn't think what I offered was good enough, is it?
- Will anyone think so?

If you thought you knew what mattered to you when you got married, when the relationship ends, you may feel unsure: What matters to me now?

Divorce invites you to show up to your life in new ways. It challenges your ideas of what really matters. It presents you with the opportunity to revisit what you have to give—and need to give—to feel fulfilled and whole. Perhaps most importantly, divorce allows you to forge a special relationship with yourself and become your own refuge. In connecting with your inner sanctuary, you create a refuge where you can be nurtured regardless of what may be happening in the outer world. Your inner sanctuary is the invisible safety net that is there as you navigate the gray space between what you are letting go and where you are going.

What Comprises Your Inner Sanctuary?

The word sanctuary comes from sanctus, meaning holy. Its original definition was "the inmost recess or holiest part of a temple or church."

If your body is the temple, think about what is inside. What comprises your sanctuary? There are the core values that define and inform how you need to live. There are your dreams of what you hope is possible. There is self-confidence built upon a foundation of successfully surviving other transitions. There is self-compassion that acknowledges you are good and whole despite mistakes you may have made. There is the belief that you are loveable. There is resilience from being humbled by disappointment. There is serenity in knowing things will work out and you will rise again.

You may have travelled far from this place during your marriage, and depending upon the nature of your divorce, it may feel farther still as you endure the emotionally bruising process. As your marriage unraveled, you may have become increasingly disconnected from yourself. You may have even abandoned yourself in a valiant attempt to save the *us*. If you subjugated *me* to *we* during your relationship, it may feel extremely scary to now just be *me*. Who are you? It may feel unnatural to focus on you. There is empty space hanging there that used to be filled with thoughts, effort, and time spent on your ex. If your spouse was abusive, you may have surrendered your self-respect and your self-esteem.

So how do you get back? How do you reconnect with yourself if you got lost along the way?

First, recognize what you gave away. Then decide what you want to reclaim. Finally, focus on what you want to create.

Identify What You Gave Away

We hear both men and women complain that they lost themselves in their marriages, or that they lost their self-esteem or self-respect. Sometimes they claim their spouse took these things from them.

To feel lost is valid, but no one actually loses themselves, their self-esteem, or their self-respect. No one else can take these from you either. Through the choices we make, we either overtly or tacitly give these things away. The effects of giving away, being robbed of, or losing something are the same: You no longer possess it. But there is an important distinction between them. Losing something connotes inaction. Having something taken away indicates victimization. Giving something away, on the other hand, is active and intentional. Notice the shift of energy within yourself as you repeat the following two sentences.

"I was afraid to get into an argument, so I just went along. In the end, I didn't even know who I was."

"In not speaking my truth, I gave my power away."

As you say the first sentence, do you feel defeated? Does your voice tend to trail off at the end? As you say the second sentence, do you hear that your voice sounds a little stronger, maybe your posture has even shifted? Noting the difference is important because you need to understand your role in how you got where you are today. Is it your perception that you lost your identity, or is it your perception that through choices you made, you gave it away? Did someone take away your self-esteem and self-respect, or through weakened boundaries, did you allow someone to manipulate you until you felt like you had none left?

What was your motivation in giving away your power? Understanding your motivation will prevent you from losing yourself in another relationship. Dr. Henry Cloud and John Townsend wrote a wonderful book, *Boundaries*. In it, they list ten laws of boundaries; one or them, the Law of Motivation, focuses on the essence of why we do what we do.

Wanting to be of service is a powerful motivator. Maybe your partner is sick and asks you to go to the grocery store. You want to help, and so you go. They would do the same for you. But what if your primary motivator in going to the store is to avoid an expected angry reaction if you refuse? If they become angry with you, perhaps you will lose the relationship. To avoid painful feelings of loneliness and rejection, you go to the store. Avoidance motivators have their source in fear. Instead of being of service out of our free will, we are doing something to avoid an expected negative reaction, which, if triggered, could result in our deepest fears being realized.

Avoidance can start with very small daily decisions. Giving becomes giving in, and you become increasingly disconnected from yourself. Giving in then becomes part of the relationship dynamic. You desire to be generous and giving, but your desire is not respected or honored by your partner. Through the very best of intentions, you are now unintentionally co-creating a dynamic that doesn't nourish you.

It is not easy to see how we play a part in allowing this dynamic in our relationships. For some people, giving away their power stems from shame and fear. For others, it emanates from their desire to keep their relationship, their way of life, their sense of security and home.

It is important to investigate this with a therapist, counselor, or support group; however, it is also important that you understand and not blame yourself for being subjected to abuse either physically or emotionally. To blame yourself is to re-wound yourself.

In shifting your perception to acknowledging your own role in the dynamic, you give up seeing yourself as a victim. You are now on the road to reclaiming your identity. You are on the road to understanding that an effective relationship is about co-creating a life together. You can take back your power and begin to choose differently. The good news about being a co-creator is that you are free to create something else. What happened in your marriage does not have to be repeated. You don't need to revisit this pain in your future. Suffering isn't your destiny.

A Story from Julie

I allowed my husband to criticize and frame me in ways that were unflattering: my standards were too high, my human need for emotional connection was clingy, I was illogical, and on and on. In fact, he took what others saw as a positive attribute, my genuine curiosity about people, and subverted it into being nosy, constantly challenging why I asked the questions I did. So I began instinctively editing what I was going to say. Instead of talking as I did with my friends, I found myself prefacing a thought by saying, "This may not make sense but ..." The saving grace for me was having friendships with people who reflected back to me how I really presented. It still hurt like hell to have the person who meant the most to me attempt to devalue and frame me in ways that suited his narrative, but I let him do it, and in so doing gave a bit more of my self-respect away each time.

Decide What You Want to Reclaim

Now that you are aware of what you gave away, it is time to reclaim it. Support groups, blogs, and articles refer to personal power. What does it mean?

Power alone is influence over others. Personal power is self-mastery; it is influence over yourself. It's people's belief that through their efforts, they have the ability to influence their own destiny and outcomes in alignment with their values and vision. Personal power is related to one's feeling of self-worth and self-confidence.

As you read this, you may feel little confidence in your ability to create a fulfilling, happy life for yourself. If you were emotionally or physically abused, your self-respect, self-esteem, and self-confidence have been severely damaged. You may question whether you even deserve anything better. So where do you start your path to reclamation? Strengthen your boundaries. Consciously decide how you want to show up to your life and choose behaviors that align with who you want to be. It is time to take back your personal power, your mastery of you.

Strengthen Boundaries

Healthy boundaries are the limits we set within our relationships that separate our unique selves from others; boundaries come from a sense of self-worth. They dictate what we will and will not tolerate, and in so doing, they prevent others from abusing or manipulating us. Boundaries acknowledge that we are responsible for how we feel, think, and behave. They are flexible, allowing people to get close to us when appropriate, and they keep others at a distance when warranted. In short, healthy boundaries protect us from others' emotional overreach and, at the same time, reflect our respect for others as capable people responsible for their own lives.

There is a strong connection between self-worth and our ability to set healthy boundaries, and this connection is most apparent in our interpersonal relationships. Our sense of self is created through relationships, and relationships are where we are most vulnerable to losing our boundaries.

In the process of going through a huge relational change like divorce, we have the opportunity to reflect and learn how we have maintained or compromised our boundaries. Divorce is a fertile ground for building our sense of self-worth.

Maybe you started out in the marriage with strong boundaries and as relationship issues surfaced, your boundaries weakened. It begins subtly. You are tired after work and ignore some patronizing comments. Fearing an argument, you don't assert your need for alone time, so you go out with your spouse's friends. You may make excuses for his or her bad behavior. You may start to believe your partner's unhappiness or personal failures are your responsibility. In your role of supportive spouse, you think you need to do more to fix things.

The result is that your boundaries erode until you are out of touch with your own needs and self-worth. Since you aren't asserting yourself, your partner is continually taking what you are giving without giving back. In the extreme, you are there to facilitate your partner's life and reflect back to them how they want to be seen, but they don't see you as a person with your own identity. You feel used and drained.

In rebuilding your boundaries after your divorce, it is important to understand that boundaries are selectively permeable. They should be neither too rigid nor too loose. They should be flexible and can be open or firm when needed.

Without firm boundaries we can easily become merged or enmeshed with others, causing us to take care of them emotionally and be neglectful of our own needs. When our boundaries are too rigid, we isolate ourselves and push others away.

Feeling Safe in Your Own Skin

The first step in developing healthy boundaries is learning that no other person can provide the inner safety that you need. Some people are provided that safety in early childhood. For others of us that was not the case; however, we can learn to develop and honor who we are and our uniqueness.

Knowing ourselves in this way is essential to true intimacy and connection. As we fine-tune our awareness, we can know own needs, desires, and preferences more fully.

Taking the time and space for your inner work is an important form of self-care, and it reinforces a deep sense of integrity. As we do this work, and continue to realize our true worth, we are less willing to tolerate the people, circumstances, and situations in our lives that do not reflect our worth and self-respect.

It is a paradox that the more centered and grounded we are in our own inner sense of self, the better partners and friends we are able to become. Working with a counselor, therapist, or support group can help you establish and maintain the boundaries you need to form effective relationships.

Surrounding yourself with positive, healthy people will accelerate your healing process and provide the supportive network you need to move through a very difficult experience. Evaluate your current relationships. Do you have people in your life who usurp your time, deplete your energy, project onto you, or are excessively needy? Consider opting to only keep the people who show through their behavior that they respect who you are and what you have to offer.

Boundaries with Yourself

While evaluating your relationships with other people, check in with the status of the relationship you have with yourself. Do you have internal limits in place that disallow torrents of negative thoughts and anxiety to invade your every waking moment? Without internal boundaries, you can sabotage and abuse yourself as easily as another person can. If you allow negative thoughts, emotions, or fears to invade your head like unruly children in a candy store, you need to impose some limits. Of course it is normal to have anxiety about your future and the current stresses that face you. You can expect to cycle through feeling sad, angry, and disappointed. But you have control over the amount of space you allow your anxiety and fear to take.

Daniel Goleman, renowned for his work in emotional intelligence and the author of *Focus: The Hidden Driver of Excellence*, describes two forms of thought: rumination and constructive worry. He defines rumination as thought loops that one can't stop and are upsetting. You keep thinking about the same things over and over again, becoming more anxious and getting nowhere. Constructive worry on the other hand is when you think about something upsetting, but you come up with something you can do about it and that stops the thought. You can then move forward and focus upon something else.

Consider consciously allocating an amount of time each day in which you will allow yourself to embrace your feelings, fears, and anxiety. Use this time to acknowledge what you are feeling without judgment. Give yourself permission to just be in that space, but at the end of the allotted time, turn your attention to another area in your life and fully engage—be it with another person, your job, or an interest. It is not that you are finished worrying about whatever it is that causes you to feel anxious, but you are taking control of anxiety's power over you by giving it only so much space in your life.

A Story from Julie

I had a client who was riddled with fears and anxiety due to many unfortunate life circumstances converging at once. She felt out of control. Negative thoughts were consuming more and more space and she was becoming increasingly more stressed, unable to move forward. We did an exercise in which she learned how to intentionally choose what to focus upon and in so doing, she became empowered, able to regain control over her emotions. You can try this if you feel you are engaged in rumination versus constructive worry.

Visualize wrapping your negative thoughts, worries and anxieties in a package and placing this "worry package" on a shelf. You are permitted to unwrap the package twice a day for a defined amount of time – she and I agreed upon one half hour. At the end of the allotted time, replace the package on the shelf to be revisited later. When the package is on the shelf, you need to focus on other things and people in your life - work, friends and interests. Eventually you will need to revisit the worry package less and less as the energy devoted to other thoughts, people, and activities begin to consume a larger space in your head and heart.

It is a process, so be patient, but also be mindful. We can't control the thoughts and feelings that come to us, but a huge measure of reclaiming personal power lies in choosing what to focus upon and realizing that it is a choice and yours to make. The good news is that focus, like resilience and optimism can be developed. As Goleman writes: "Think of attention as a mental muscle that we can strengthen by a workout."

Focus on Creating

We are each gifted in a unique and important way. It is our privilege and our adventure to discover our own special light.

—MARY DUNBAR

As you begin to reclaim your personal power, you start to have more energy available to create. As the divorce process becomes a more distant memory and you move away from crisis management mode, a powerful energy shift occurs. Creation is energizing because it is positive and expansive. What do you want to create for yourself moving forward? Now is the time to be intentional. You have an opportunity and the ability to create a new you, a new life with anything and anyone you want in it. You don't need to accommodate or attempt to please your spouse anymore. Yes, this new life is scary, but it is also liberating.

You may choose to develop a new friendship with someone you only peripherally know but admire. You may book a trip to somewhere you have always longed to go. Maybe you'll take cooking lessons or learn a new language. Be imaginative. Reward yourself for taking back your life. Don't focus on the resources and action steps that will be necessary to support each idea right now; just let your inner voice speak.

Revisit what makes you unique. Once you recognize what makes you unique and valuable, you can share your gift with others. This is a time in your life filled with opportunity. You have the prospect for greater happiness, an occasion to explore who you are (maybe for the first time), and a chance to meet someone who will really deserve what you have to give and will honor who you are.

Exercises

1. Recognizing what I gave away: my story about personal power.

Write down everything you feel you lost or surrendered during your marriage—include everything big and small, from your sense of self-esteem and self-confidence to hobbies or interests. Reread what you wrote. Are you blaming your spouse? Now rewrite this narrative being intentional. How did you give these things away? How did you co-create the situation in which you find yourself today?

2. What do I want to reclaim?

Look at your rewritten narrative from the previous exercise. Of all the things you gave away, which ones do you want back in your life? You are a different person now than when you got married, so make a conscious choice about what people, attributes, and interests best serve who you are today and who you want to be. There may be relationships, interests, or hobbies that no longer serve you, so you can leave them behind.

Next to each item that you want to reclaim, list one small action you can take that would move you closer. For example, if you want a better sense of self-esteem, what small thing could you do that would start to rebuild it—volunteer, exercise each day?

3. How am I showing up?

List all the important pieces of your life: children, other family members, friends, job, and anything else that matters to you. Next to each item listed, consider how well you feel you are showing up. On a scale of 1 to 10, with 10 being "fully present" and 1 being "absent," score yourself. In any area in which you scored less than an 8, list some changes you could make that would increase your score. You aren't aiming for huge steps, but rather small shifts.

For example, if you scored yourself a 2 in one area, aim to get it to a 4 not an 8. You can come back again when you are at a 4. Commit to making small changes in the next month and set a date on the calendar in thirty days when you will come back and re-examine the list, update the ratings, and repeat the process as necessary.

4. What do I want to create?

Envision yourself in the future looking back on your life. What does a life well lived look like in terms of family, career, community, and other vital elements? Write down what you see. Don't censor yourself. You're not creating goals in this exercise. You are only looking ahead to what you would like to see in your life.

Step 6:
Decide

Act "As If"

Once you make a decision, the world conspires to make it happen.

—Ralph Waldo Emerson

Every transformation begins with a decision. In this case, the decision you make changes the course of your life. Coming to the point of decision is about becoming more aware that you have a choice. You can call upon your internal sense of determination, humor, and even a positive sense of reproach.

A Story from Judy

During a long meditation retreat at Spirit Rock Meditation Center, I was having a series of panic attacks. I imagined that a fierce dog was snarling and foaming at the mouth just off to the side in the corner of my eye on the edge of my line of vision. I would dream about this dog and it would follow me into my sittings. It was, of course, a metaphor for the anxiety that I carried.

I went for an interview with my teacher, Jack Kornfield. I told him about my predicament, expecting lots of sympathy and compassion. Instead he said, "Looks like you have a new pet." I laughed and laughed. In that moment, the dog disappeared along with my anxiety, and I realized that I had a choice. I could carry it around or I could decide to own my life and move out of the anxiety.

Pema Chödrön quotes her teacher in the same way. Chödrön was prone to panic attacks and told her teacher, Chogyam Trungpa Rinpoche, about her anxiety. He said in a compassionate but firm way, "Do you want to keep having panic attacks or do you want to wake up?" It was a gentle reproach that did a world of good.

Do you want to feel stuck in your sadness, anxiety, and despair or do you want to free yourself and wake up? Use discernment. You need to grieve and be sad for a while, but you will intuitively know when it's time to wake up and decide to own your life.

This is a pivotal point. You don't have to waste years getting over your divorce. It's important to be present with your pain and emotions initially, but so many people get stuck in the mud of resentment, depression, and disappointment. This is not your path! It's not necessary.

As painful as it may be to admit that your marriage is at an end, sometimes ending a painful or difficult marriage is the only way you can empower yourself to move forward toward a state of emotional health and growth. Once you have made the transition, you will find that you are open to new experiences and new relationships that never seemed possible before. If your marriage has been demeaning, damaging to your self-esteem, painful, or even boring, take comfort in the knowledge that divorce may signify the beginning of something, not the end.

By deciding, you are embracing your power to make your own way, to reclaim your life. This is a confidence builder. There is power in making this decision. By creating this dynamic in your life, you are starting an upward cycle of confident, self-owning behaviors.

There is power in focusing on your relationship to a situation rather focusing on the situation itself. When you do this you become more aware of your responses and habitual patterns of thinking. You can see the opportunities open to you if you think a different way, and your confidence will grow.

Deciding is not about whether to leave the marriage or not. If you are reading this book, you have already made that decision or someone has made it for you. The decision we are talking about is to embrace your life and live the best life possible—to allow this painful time to transform you into the being you were meant to be.

Removing Obstacles and Clearing the Path

As you go through the process of moving on with your life, you've got to clear some things out of the way. Bitterness, resentment, and anger have their place, but not in your new life. They will only hold you back. Take the power back by saying to yourself: I can't help what happened to me, but I can change how I react to what happened to me. That gives you the power back.

Pray, meditate, and find a way to get a clear picture of how your decision will turn out over a lifetime. Ask yourself what success looks like for you.

An Important Checklist on Deciding

Your decision is real. It's not just a wish or something hoped for. It is visceral and made with your whole mind and body. Have you truly decided? Have you made a commitment to yourself to have the best life you can possibly have?

Without distractions, you will be able to hear what is most important to you. What is trying to speak to you? You may remember in the movie *The Color Purple*, as Shug sings in the juke joint and hears the church choir, she makes a decision to go to the church and meet her father. In this moving scene of forgiveness, she is reunited with her father as the choir sings: "God is trying to tell you something." Perhaps the divine in you is trying to tell you something now.

Thought Questions

- **What and who do you need to forgive?**

- **How can you decide to learn to respond rather than react? Responding suggests thoughtfulness, patience, and wisdom. Reacting is being a victim to your emotions.**

- **Embrace the idea of a new lens. How you see your world will change your life. Assigning blame and making excuses continues the cycle of victimization. Yes, your spouse acted in a terrible way and devastated you. How long do you want to use your energy on** something that will not be part of your future? It's not hurting your former loved one; it's hurting you. You can't make a powerful decision to create a new life and still remain a victim.

- It is important to move from the state of wishing to the state of decision. A wish is something that would be nice if all the stars aligned and it happened. A decision is a firm state of resolve that closes the door marked "What am I going to do?" and opens a new door marked "How am I going to do it?"

Exercise

Set a date to decide. Put it in your calendar. Go to a secluded and quiet space. It could be a nearby beach or forest, or you could rent a cabin or hotel room. Give yourself permission to be by yourself. Allow yourself to sit quietly, even meditate. Be open to all thoughts as they come to you. Don't hold on to any thoughts. Allow them to come and go. Don't blame yourself; don't blame others. Realize that this is your one wild and precious life. Don't waste another moment wishing for things to be different. Accept life; accept reality as it is.

Use a journal or some blank sheets of paper to create the life you want.

- First, envision the life you want. Write a paragraph at the top of your page. Be as specific as possible. For example, "I want to have two new friends by the end of this year. I want to have a romantic relationship that is kind and caring. This will happen in __ months. I want to be living in _____ by the end of _____."

- Next, write a paragraph that describes your current reality at the bottom of the page. Leave the middle of the page blank. For example: "I have been divorced for two months. I am depressed and lack energy. I keep thinking of my ex and being sad. I have two wonderful children. I have a job I like." Be real, and put down what is true for you.

- Explore the gap between these by writing down the steps you need to take to get from your current reality to your vision.

- Finally, make a decision to move on and change your attitude. Begin the journey to your new life on the date you set for yourself.

Act "As If"

Drum sounds rise on the air,
and with them, my heart.
A voice inside the beat says,
I know you are tired, but come.
This is the way.

—RUMI

One of the biggest myths is that we have to feel like doing something before we do it. As you go through divorce, you might tell yourself that you have to feel like making new friends, dating, changing your habits, exercising, and many other things. Nothing could be further from the truth. The old adage says, "Seeing is believing," but the opposite is true: "Believing is seeing." So many of us have the silent mantra of "I'll believe it when I see it." In doing so, we hold ourselves back, limit what's possible, and negate the power of our minds, imaginations, and intentions to create new, unpredictable, and even miraculous experiences and outcomes.

One of America's pioneering psychologists, William James, said that the greatest discovery is that we as human beings can alter our lives simply by altering our attitudes of mind. He advocated that if you act as if you are what you want to be, you will become that.

The ABC Theory of Emotion asserts the same idea. It represents a widely accepted model of how one's feelings and behavioral patterns are created. It says that the emotions we experience and their resulting behavior do not come directly from the events in our lives, but from our interpretations of events—that is, emotions come from conscious or subconscious beliefs we bring to situations. The theory is rooted in Rational-EmotiveTherpy (RET) developed initially by Albert

Ellis. According to Ellis, more than 200 research articles confirm this theory.

Still another great thinker, German philosopher Hans Vaihinger, wrote a book called *The Philosophy of 'As If.'* This is where the saying, "Fake it till you make it" comes from. If you don't feel confident, pretend you are until you gain the experience or tools to make your confidence real. Therapists use this idea all the time for patient's suffering from depression. Although it might feel artificial and forced in the beginning, soon it will become more natural until you are happier and healthier.

No one feels competent one hundred percent of the time, but they press on. We often get exactly what we expect, which is a pretty powerful concept if we take time to let it in and live with that awareness. Instead of waiting to see how things turn out, hoping that they will get better, or simply allowing the circumstances and situations in our lives to determine how we feel, what if we acted as if we had everything within us and around us that we need to be successful, happy, and fulfilled already—which we do, by the way!

Any decent athlete, salesman, or Starbucks barista can put on a good game face. Act as if goes much deeper than thinking positively. It's a method, a learned skill, for convincing your mind that you already are what you want to become. The body follows where the mind leads.

A Story from Judy

When clients come into my office, it's usually because they want to feel better. They want to have a better life and understand what limits them. They want to be less sad, less anxious, more self-confident, or less angry.

First, I ask them to create the life they want on paper.

> After this is written down, then I ask them to describe their current reality. Then I ask them to describe how a person would act if they had already achieved the ideal life they wrote about. In doing this, they are able to describe the behaviors they would need to adopt in getting from their current reality to the life they want. Perhaps it would mean acting as if they were confident or acting as if they were attractive to the opposite sex. Perhaps they want to be more responsible and caring. They don't need to feel more responsible and caring; they needed to start acting that way. The feelings follow the action.

As an experiment, act as if you cannot fail. Act as if you have the love of your life. Act as if you have a steady stream of income. Act as if you are in shape and have good health. Even though you may feel awkward at assuming these behaviors, you will be shocked at how you can create self-fulfilling prophecies.

Acting as if works in a number of different ways. Instead of dwelling on the negative, which typically makes us feel worse, acting as if things were how you would like them allows you to focus on the positive. It takes your focus off yourself and puts it more on creating what you want.

Noted Harvard psychology professor Ellen Langer has conducted many high-profile experiments using the act as if principle. She and her graduate students studied the biological impact of acting as if on a group of elderly men. A control group of older men were told that they would attend a retreat where they would spend a week reminiscing about the past; the experimental group, by contrast, would spend a week surrounded by paraphernalia from twenty years earlier, listening to radio shows and discussing news from the period. They were not allowed to bring up any events that happened after 1959, and they were to refer to themselves, their families, and their careers as they were at that time.

The point was not living in the past; rather, it was about giving mental signals to the body to reflect the energy and biological responses of a much younger person. By acting as if they were younger, the men in the experimental group actually changed their performance on benchmark tests. At the end of the study, the experimental group demonstrated marked improvement in hearing, eyesight, memory, dexterity, and appetite. Some who had arrived using canes, dependent on the aid of their children, walked out under their own power, carrying their own suitcases. Langer concluded that by expecting them to function independently and engaging with them as individual minds rather than as old people, she and her students gave them the opportunity to see themselves differently. This, then, had an impact on them biologically.

This study was called the Counterclockwise, and it showed the power of possibilities. If the mind could have such an impact on the body, what other potential might exist in terms of healing? How important are the words that doctors use when talking with patients or that patients use about their disease? Langer has continued to study mindfulness and its effects.

A Story from Judy

I was lucky in my life to have a grandmother who epitomized Langer's study without even understanding the theory. Gracie, who died at 96, was always young, especially in her own mind. She loved adventures and helping others. In her eighties she volunteered to help the senior citizens of her church. She would take food and help do errands for

> people twenty years her junior. She took Jazzercise at ninety-one. She didn't like to be called grandma; she preferred Gracie. She loved having parties and having fun. She gave me the advice of never telling my age. She said, "People will limit you and treat you differently if they know how old you are." How right she was.

Imagine using the same principle that Langer studied. You are a happy person, excited by the future, looking forward to what life brings. How would acting as if this were true change your current circumstances and change your life? How would people respond to you in this mental state?

Old mental models can limit you in your transition after divorce. Shift these patterns of thinking into acting as if you are the opposite.

Exercise 1

Take a pen and paper and write down ways you can avoid these mental traps.

I am a failure because my marriage didn't work.
No matter the circumstances of your breakup, do you have a nagging feeling that you have failed? Reaize that you may be uncomfortable not because your marriage failed, but because you believe you are a failure. You carry that energy around, and everyone else can feel it. In turn they may treat you like a failure or feel sorry for you. Only you can turn this around. You made the choice to believe you are a failure and to feel like a failure. The mental model of failure does

not serve you. It has never helped anyone lead a happy life.

You have the ability to control that mind-set and to act as if you are something else. What would that be? Putting yourself in this new frame of mind may feel uncomfortable and awkward at first; however, your feelings will eventually catch up to your new way of thinking. Making this choice is solely up to you.

I want revenge.

When you are stuck in blaming your ex or the other woman or man, you are keeping yourself stuck in the pain. Revenge may seem great, but it only contains negative feelings and it prevents you from moving on to a better life. Having fantasies of how you will get back at him or her will only keep you feeling bad and in the self-talk of pain and blame.

What would be the opposite of revenge? How could you act as if? Ultimately the best medicine for revenge is living a happy and fulfilling life.

I feel sorry for myself.

Unfortunately, going through a divorce makes us susceptible to having pity parties for ourselves. We want our friends and loved ones to know how miserable we are. Eventually even the best of friends get weary. If you keep yourself in this state of pity, you will have a hard time moving on to your new life.

What would your new mental model be? What is the opposite of feeling sorry for yourself?

I feel frightened of being alone.

A huge gift in going through the transition of your divorce is to get reintroduced to yourself. There is an enormous amount of love waiting for you: the love you feel for yourself. This is an opportunity to reawaken your relationship with yourself. Somehow you got lost in the marriage and forgot who you are. You let the struggles of the relationship mask what you felt for yourself. Perhaps it is time to embark on a spiritual journey with yourself.

The quality of your life is completely dependent on the quality of your relationship with you.

I'm strong so I don't need help.

Getting outside help doesn't mean you are not strong. Getting perspective from someone wise is a healthy move. Even if it's just one hour a week, you will feel invigorated by space to talk and not wallow in your misery.

Exercise 2

Think about the negative beliefs you have about this change and what has happened to you. Write about or paint the person who walks around everyday with these beliefs. What does he or she look like? Look in the mirror and describe his or her face in five years. How does it feel? Who are his or her friends? What sort of person does he or she attract?

You have the opportunity now to change this. You have the opportunity to do the work to create a wonderful future.

Step 7:
Build a New Story

Create A New Perspective

In the long run, we shape our lives, and we shape ourselves. The process never ends until we die. And the choices we make are ultimately our own responsibility.
—Eleanor Roosevelt

To construct a story of our lives is to make meaning of it.

A Story from Judy

I remember as a young mother I took my two small girls to the beach along with two other mothers. We were all set for a day in the sun. The kids were so excited. The other two mothers each had a little boy, both about three years old.

We set our things up on the beach, then each mom took the hand of her little boy. It was the first time for both boys to be at the beach and to see the enormous ocean. They giggled and laughed as they stepped into the water. Wading

92

> out a little farther, they tiptoed and jumped as small waves covered their feet.
>
> Suddenly a larger, unexpected wave came crashing in. The boys were doused. They came up sputtering. The moms laughed and kept hold of the boys' hands. One little boy started laughing and jumping, so thrilled by the unexpected feeling of being rolled by the wave. The other little boy was screaming and fighting, obviously terrified by the experience.

How can two people have different experiences of the same event?

When divorce happens, it is natural to feel in pain, betrayed, and bitter. The belief you have about your divorce is what makes the pain last and the suffering continue. Just as the two little boys had differing experiences in the ocean, in divorce, some people recover and go on to happy and creative lives while others never recover and will remain angry and bitter. Why is that?

It's simple and not so simple. We do not suffer from what happens to us, but we suffer from what we believe about what happens to us. Our emotions and motivation comes from the story that we believe about ourselves and our lives.

That is not to say that going through a divorce or other traumatic event is not painful or disappointing, but the pain and disappointment can last a long time and be dysfunctional because of the story you tell yourself about what has happened to you.

There is a saying: "What do fish talk about? Certainly not water." We swim around in our own stories, believing what we think to be true is in fact true. We do not understand that we have the power to change those beliefs, thereby making our lives much happier and effective.

Yes, he left me. Yes, he was cruel. Yes, he found someone else. Does this justify a story that keeps you sad and embittered for years? It doesn't matter what the actual facts are, it matters what you create as a story to live by in your life. These stories and beliefs have a huge impact on the way we feel and interact with others. We understand the world by making it up. "We tell ourselves stories in order to live," as Joan Didion famously put it.

Personal narratives are stories we hold onto about ourselves. The primary function of a story is to make sense of our worlds. Although we sometimes tell these stories to others to manage the impression we present, its primary function is to help create order out of the chaos of life, especially during difficult times.

Dan P. McAdams, a professor of psychology at Northwestern and author of *The Redemptive Self*, states: "We find that these narratives guide behavior in every moment, and frame not only how we see the past but how we see ourselves in the future." By changing the story, what happened to you in the past does not determine what your life can be in the future.

This thinking resonates with a favorite quote of mine: "Whatever harm has been done to you is the least important thing about you." That is a good beginning to a new story!

A better story for yourself leads to more creativity, options, and hope for your life. Being more creative in developing a story that works for you makes you more likely to be energetic and involved. McAdams writes: "Generative people ... tend to see many of the events in their life in the reverse order, as linked by themes of redemption. They flunked sixth grade but met a wonderful counselor and made honor roll in seventh. They were laid low by divorce, only to meet a wonderful new partner."

Even though it's hard to find and hold your center during divorce, you must begin the work of grounding yourself and beginning the journey back to your center. In the work of changing your story or mind-set, be quiet and really ask what is important to you. Who are you? What do you believe? What is important to you as a human being?

Now ask yourself: How connected do I feel? How connected am I to myself? How connected am I to the world and people around me? What can I own and be responsible for in my emotional life? For instance, have you been looking to or depending on someone else to make you happy? If so, you need a different mind-set, a new lens to live your life and love yourself.

What is your story about what has happened to you? What do you tell yourself? Are you aware of the story by which you are living? Do you notice a pattern—do the words and tone seem familiar? Become more aware of what you are telling yourself and how that impacts your life.

Many people use divorce as a reason to feel sorry for themselves and to remain bitter. It's hard to combat the fact that a hard and painful thing has happened; however, it is even harder for your friends and loved ones to tell you that you are hanging on to a victim stance and becoming less effective in your life.

Thought Questions

Are you telling a victim's story? See if you can detect your story by asking yourself these questions.

- **How do people react when you tell your story about what happened? Do they seem awkward? Do they change the subject? Pay attention and listen to the effect you are having.**

- **Does your belief and story help you feel motivated and look forward to life?**

- **Do you want to give up?**

- Does your story make you feel fatigued and tired?

- Are you hopeful about your life?

- Does the story help you feel better about yourself as a person?

- What would you think if you listened to your story as an unbiased observer?

Remember these truths as you begin building a better story for your life.

- The situation you are in is the least important thing about you.

- You are not the problem; the problem is the problem.

- Your self-doubt is not a measure of your own self-worth.

- Take one hundred percent responsibility for your own life.

- Own up to your actions. Not doing this takes away your ability to do anything different. You remain stuck while you continue to complain and feel miserable in a story of negativity.

- You may in fact be the recipient of external forces outside your control, but you have control over your reactions and responses.

- When you look at what has happened through the lens of "What can I learn from this?" you are creating a story that will serve you all of your life.

- Most people believe that there is something basically wrong with them. Is this part of your story?

- **You are basically good; your true nature is one of goodness and kindness. You just have to create the story of how you live your life to unlock this truth.**

Exercise

Find a quiet place, take out your journal and pretend that your life is a book—a very interesting and complex book. It is full of joys and sorrows. You have just finished reading a chapter full of sorrow, pain, and tension. Now write the next several chapters about how you came through this time in your life and what grew out of it.

Step 8:
Forgive (or Not)

Move On

The weak can never forgive. Forgiveness is the attribute of the strong.

—MAHATMA GANDHI

See if you can relate to the following sentiment:

"There have been times when just the thought of forgiving my ex brought up such rage that I thought I would explode. There have been times when I have been sure that it was impossible to forgive."

Anger and rage usually cover up feelings of loss, betrayal, unworthiness, heartbreak, and vulnerability. All of these feelings need the cool waters of healing. If you hold onto anger, it is impossible to heal the hurt that's beneath it. So why is it that we often keep grudges and animosity, sometimes for years or even a lifetime? Why do we recycle unpleasant circumstances in our minds and keep those wounds open?

We want to protect ourselves. Our egos want to keep us safe.

So if a past situation has hurt us, ego likes to replay it over and over, keeping the memory and feelings alive to prevent the same situation from occurring again—but preventing future pain doesn't work that way. By holding onto the grudge, we're actually keeping those wounds wide open, fueling the flames of the negative emotions, and causing even more pain. And if you are dwelling in negative energy, you are less likely to attract what you want in your life.

Forgiveness is the capacity to let go; it is the ability to release the suffering, sorrows, and burdens of the pains and betrayals of the past that devour your energy, leaving you with inadequate resources to move forward. And until you forgive, you still have an emotional foot in the past, and you are trapped inside a broken relationship.

As Nobel laureate Elie Wiesel writes: "Suffering confers neither privileges nor rights. It all depends on how you use it. If you use it to increase the anguish of yourself or others, you are degrading, even betraying it. Yet the day will come when we shall understand that suffering can also elevate human beings. God help us to bear our suffering well."

Forgiveness involves a shift of identity. Each of us has an undying capacity for love and freedom that is untouched by what happens to us, and to come back to this true nature is the work of forgiveness.

Letting go is a choice. Forgiveness does not free the other person; it frees you. When we hold onto hurt feelings, it is the ego's response to a person or situation. When we hold on to the hurt, we are giving that person power over us.

For some, it is not possible to forgive in this moment, and that is OK. You can still move forward by placing the intention to forgive in your heart. This does not mean you condone or validate the behavior of your ex. It means that you are on the journey of freeing yourself from unhappiness and pain.

The intent to forgive is a powerful tool, and choosing it is the first step to freeing yourself. Even though your feelings are still hurt, create the intention to let new feelings come in. Encourage even the slightest hints of a new feeling. Unhappiness is solitary; healing is not.

Forgiveness, even the intent to forgive, is not always so easy to put into practice. If somebody wrongs us, why should they be let off the hook for being awful? What about how they made you feel?   But forgiving somebody does not mean that what they did is OK or that you are going to be friends with them. It just means that you are releasing them and are no longer going to let them have any control over you, your feelings, or your energy.

When you set your intention, it sets the compass of your heart and your psyche. By having that intention, even if you are not able to fully forgive, obstacles become surmountable because you know where you are going.

Another way to set the intention to forgive is to be grateful for what you have learned. Every situation in our lives, especially the negative ones, can teach us something. Not being able to forgive is an important, deep lesson. It is the sort of potential major a-ha moment or awakening waiting to happen. Set your intention and be ready to receive the lesson. Be grateful for the opportunity to learn and grow.

There is a life force that pushes grass up through the sidewalk. The same force is in you. When you listen deeply, ask: What is my best intention? Set the intention to let go and trust that it will happen.

A Story from Julie

When I forgave my ex, it came in the form of a quiet realization that although he hurt me terribly, he could do no better. That is who he was and where he was while we were married. I believe he loved me to the flawed extent that was possible for him. It wasn't an adequate love. It wasn't a giving or a mature love, but it was all he had to offer. Ultimately I had accepted it and pretended it was enough. So I forgave myself as well, because that is who and where I was at the time.

This realization set me free because I accepted my ex and his limitations, and I acknowledged my own role in the failed dynamic. This acceptance released me from the land of *whys* and *how could yous.*

There is no one-size-fits-all timeline. And you can't will forgiveness to happen. It is a process like everything else, and it is tied to your readiness to let go. Everyone who goes through a breakup is on his or her own schedule. It is extremely difficult to get to forgiveness if you are recovering from betrayal and feelings of rejection, so be patient with yourself. You may need to create an intention to forgive before you actually get to a place where you can forgive.

Exploring Definitions of Forgiveness

Our ability to forgive and let go of the anger may in part depend upon our definitions of forgiveness. There is not just one universal meaning that rings true for everyone. Definitions vary among dictionaries and publications.

Here is the definition from the Mayo Clinic: "Generally, forgiveness is a decision to let go of resentment and thoughts of revenge. ... Forgiveness can even lead to feelings of understanding, empathy, and compassion for the one who hurt you."

For many people, the idea of putting anger and resentment behind them is a difficult concept to embrace when the hurt is raw. And feeling anger is actually helpful in your transition as it allows you to emotionally separate from your ex. In the early part of your divorce transition, anger is good. It helps you move forward and is a necessary part of the grief cycle. You need to acknowledge it and express it.

However, anger that lingers past your divorce and consumes a significant amount of energy becomes self-defeating. It holds you back. To get beyond it, consider different meanings around forgiveness.

Jack Kornfield offers this definition: "Forgiveness means giving up our hope that the past could have been any different." This takes the emphasis off your ex and puts it with you and your disappointed hope. It also brings us to the present and it implicitly offers the question, "Now what?" which invites a look to the future.

We have so much vested in this past, so many things we thought we wanted—and isn't that what really keeps us so hooked to hurt? We want to rescript the past to fit our dreams, what we thought was possible, what we believed was possible when we walked down the aisle. We become obsessed with resisting the unhappy ending.

Are you ready to go out on a limb? What if you actually said, "My marriage ended and so what?" It doesn't have to be a tragedy of Shakespearean proportions. It could be a simple tale of two people who worked for a while and then they didn't. When the relationship no longer served one or both people, it ended. Leaving the past behind opens you to possibility and empowerment. What will you do?

Self-Forgiveness

None of us intentionally make decisions that end in disappointment, but it happens to everyone. It could be a job that didn't work out, a financial deal that went south, a friend who let you down, or a marriage that ended in divorce. There is value in pausing after these occurrences to appreciate the teachable moments and grasp the takeaways, so that we can be better informed for future decisions.

However, there is no value in engaging in unproductive thought loops that ask "How did I not see this coming?" or "How could I be so stupid?" This kind of thinking leads to paralysis and shame. If you are indulging these thoughts, how can you to lighten up?

It is not a reflection of your intellect that the partner you chose wasn't the right one for you. Even if there were red flags that you should have seen, you still didn't make a bad decision. You can only see what you are ready to see. Personal evolution cannot be forced into a convenient timetable. Each of us makes the decisions we do with who we are and with the information available to us at the time. Nothing is definite and people and circumstances are constantly changing.

The good news is that even if you didn't get the outcome you hoped for, the experience is not wasted. Maybe you have children you love with that person. Maybe you shared some wonderful experiences that will give you pleasure to remember in future years when you get past the pain. Some of the most difficult people in our lives are our most valuable teachers. What have you learned about yourself?

So let go of the shame. Give yourself a well-deserved break and join the rest of us—millions of us who also didn't choose a partner with whom we could grow old. We are a fun group, comprised of bright, successful, appealing people, and we don't judge others for the decisions they made that didn't turn out well because each of us have been there.

And if you were the one who through your behavior caused the marriage to end, you need to forgive yourself. Feeling ashamed or endlessly punishing yourself is not going to help your ex, and it certainly will not help you grow. In fact, the worse your self-image, the longer it will take to recover from your divorce. There is a lot of grace in just owning your own mess and saying (even if just to yourself), "I was not the person I wanted to be and I didn't show up to my marriage in the way I wish I had. I know I can be better and I will commit to that going forward."

Everyone screws up. Owning your mistakes with a determination to do better takes courage and strength of character, and it is a step toward reclaiming self-respect. Everyone deserves the chance to do better.

If you are having trouble forgiving yourself instead of punishing yourself consider ways you can productively exorcise your guilt. Do a good act for someone else. Helping others is a healthy way to feel better, and when you can like yourself, you can form more meaningful relationships.

Exercises

1. What is one step you can take to forgive yourself? How could you give yourself a break?

2. Are you at a point where you can forgive or let go? What needs to happen for you to get there? What would be possible for you if you could let go?

3. Write the definition of "forgiveness" that works for you.

4. For those of you not ready to forgive, how can you move forward? What small steps can you take? What support do you need in place to do this?

Step 9:
Turn Abandonment
into Self-Love

Resilience

For far too long we have been seduced into walking a path that did not lead us to ourselves. For far too long we have said yes when we wanted to say no. And for far too long we have said no when we desperately wanted to say yes. ... When we don't listen to our intuition, we abandon our souls. And we abandon our souls because we are afraid if we don't, others will abandon us.

—TERRY TEMPEST WILLIAMS

You are alone: That is all too painfully clear. The mind can make countless stories about this fact. Understanding the story that you create about your aloneness is key to successfully crossing the ocean of your recovery to an abundant and fulfilling life.

This is tricky because many of us have suffered, really suffered from a sense of abandonment. Whether you are left or the one leaving, the old voices raise themselves in your psyche, the ones that have never quite left. Now that you are alone, this proves—or so these voices say—that you are not good enough, that you are not worthy.

Maybe your feelings of abandonment have deep roots—your dad left or was just not there for you; your mom was indifferent or too tired to pay much attention to you. You feel guilty because you recognize your childhood was really not so bad; it could have been worse. Yet you have those nagging, dark feelings of abandonment, shame, and being not quite good enough.

There is good news here. As you recover from this divorce you have a profound opportunity to do some deep healing. You have the opportunity to transform your sense of abandonment into the gift of self-love.

There are two kinds of abandonment: physical and emotional. Physical abandonment is self-explanatory. Emotional abandonment is even more devastating. You undoubtedly experienced loss and pain at the ending of your marriage. If you were the one left, you most likely have felt the brunt of that abandonment and pain. If you are the one who left, then the guilt of that and the feelings of shame may be intense. Why does it hurt so much when someone leaves us?

Abandonment is a primal fear. The first fear that each of us experience as an infant is the fear that we will be left, literally abandoned, with no one to care for us. As children, we depend on our caretakers to be there no matter what mistakes we make or how we present ourselves to the world. In orphanages where there is no primary care taker, this syndrome is called "failure to thrive". Babies who are not emotionally connected and are not emotionally nurtured become depressed and lethargic. Their development is hindered and sometimes they may even die.

These primal fears lay deep in the limbic brain. We may be surprised by the force and pain triggered when we experience a feeling of abandonment.

Abandonment is similar to grief, but it is complicated by rejection and betrayal. This can be very confusing. Most often we turn that rage and anger against ourselves. This in turn can lead to depression, often a very deep and painful depression. When we think that the breakup was due in part to our own failings, our own inadequacies, then we start the downward spiral of abandoning ourselves.

If not addressed, this insecurity can sabotage our lives and future relationships. The fear of being left makes it more difficult to let go. In a relationship, this can look like neediness and dependence.

This is a common story or mental model that we adopt. It is an old story, a childish story. The reason it feels so childish and small is that we created it in our family of origin as a child. We didn't have adult tools to look at the whole picture.

All we knew is that we were small and that we didn't feel love from those people on whom we depended.

As you relive this childhood story, you may experience intense emotional pain and feel as helpless as you did as a child. These feelings are part of a story, and it is necessary to change that story for your growth and recovery. Just as grief has its stages, the story of your abandonment will flow through stages. These stages do not happen like steps on a ladder but often happen at the same time or over and over again.

As you journey through your divorce process, it is important to not abandon yourself. If you felt abandoned as a child, if you feel abandoned now, the key to reclaiming your wholeness is to commit to being there for yourself in a loving, compassionate way.

It is easy to feel overwhelmed even before you start, since old messages can feel deeply ingrained. But there is good news here. As you recover from divorce, you have a profound opportunity to do some deep healing of your abandonment. You have the opportunity to transform your sense of abandonment into the gift of self-love.

To shift from the old to the new, you have to write a new chapter, a new mental model. First, stop trying to make the criticism and feelings of abandonment go away. Why? What we resist persists. They are there for a reason. Somehow, as a child, it was helpful to think these things. Thinking you were unworthy helped you believe that you were in control even it was only a negative control. If you could change yourself, you might be able to get your parents' love.

Instead of scolding and criticizing these childish thoughts, it is time to re-parent, time to hold your small self and cherish who you are. It is an opportunity to become a good parent to your self.

You can't be too kind to yourself. Sometimes, people mistake self-compassion for selfishness and narcissism. The Buddha said, "If you could look at everyone in this world, you wouldn't find anyone more deserving of compassion than you."

Taking the very best care of yourself is beneficial to everyone, as you will have more love and generosity to spread around once you feel better, and feel more deserving of kindness and respect.

Temporarily escaping from your unpleasant feelings only makes them come back with a vengeance. By exploring and accepting them, they lose their power. It's almost like agreeing with someone who is looking for a fight: It takes the wind out of that person's sails. These emotional storms are part of your healing passage to a calmer and more peaceful you.

Exercise

- Write in your journal about your own story of abandonment and loss. What was it like to be the daughter or son of your parents? What messages did you get about your worth as a human being?

- Next, write about the coping tools you developed as a child to deal with feelings of abandonment. Were you shy, afraid to use your voice or talk about your feelings and opinions? What did you do to soothe yourself during this time?

- Are these coping tools still around? Write about the way you still use these tools even as an adult. Do you procrastinate? Do you overeat or drink too much? Are you critical or sarcastic of others to keep them away from you? Are you jealous or suspicious in your relationships? Are you easily hurt? Do you feel rejected when not asked to be with a group of friends or are left out of conversations at a party? Are you reassuring to others or do you wait to be reassured?

- Now write the next chapter in your life. What are the adult tools you could use in coping with archaic feelings of abandonment and shame? How can you best parent yourself?

From Fear to Resilience

Sorrow prepares you for joy. It violently sweeps every-
thing out of your house, so that new joy can find space to
enter. It shakes the yellow leaves from the bough of your
heart, so that fresh, green leaves can grow in their place.
It pulls up the rotten roots, so that new roots hidden be-
neath have room to grow. Whatever sorrow shakes from
your heart, far better things will take their place.

—RUMI

Resilience is that ineffable quality that allows some people to be knocked down by life and come back stronger than ever. Rather than letting failure overcome them and drain their resolve, they find a way to rise from the ashes.

Can resilience be learned? The answer is a resounding yes.

From research we know that resilience, also known as psychological hardiness, can be learned. My (Judy) dissertation research looked at resilience and life satisfaction in police officers. I found that police officers who witness many traumatic events were more satisfied with life if they were more psychologically hardy.

This research and numerous other studies have found three important constructs in being a more resilient person: challenge, control, and commitment.

- Challenge means seeing problems or stressors as op-portunities. Individuals with this trait accept change as part of life and don't expect it to be easy.

- Control means not seeing oneself as a helpless victim who is at the mercy of stressors. It involves having an internal locus of control, or the feeling that you can influence the course of your life and take actions that will improve your chances of achieving your goals. Individuals with this trait are generally optimistic and hopeful and feel a sense of personal power.

- Commitment is having a sense of purpose and meaning in life. Persons with this trait do not just survive, going through life with little direction. Instead they thrive.

These constructs relate to divorce: You can create opportunity out of loss. You can rewrite the story of what has happened to you, changing it from one of loss to a story of starting over in a smart way.

You have learned lessons. You can face life in a deeper more meaningful way. You understand that you cannot control other people. This is a primary but very hard lesson. Deeply understanding this will free you from blame and resentment.

Having commitment to something in your life is crucial to your well-being. Even if it's being committed to your garden, live that wholeheartedly and life will take on more meaning. In a study of Holocaust survivors, the people who were committed to something survived longer and recovered better than others.

Strength in Vulnerability

Our culture tells us that you gain power and resilience by being strong and independent. It feeds us the illusion that power is everything. But when a tree is being buffeted by the wind, the trees that survive are the ones that bend. The ones that are brittle and hard, they snap.

We believe that we are weak when we feel down and vulnerable. We force ourselves to put on a façade of strength even in the face of a tremendous loss. But there is strength in vulnerability, and there is strength in allowing the pain of loss to move you and change you.

Exercise

In your journal on three separate pages, write the words Control, Commitment and Challenge.

- **Challenge:** Think about the way you tell the story of what has happened to you in your divorce process. How can you reframe this story to present an opportunity? What stories are you telling that position you as the victim or innocent bystander? Reframe these stories with a more resilient you.

- **Control:** Who do you blame for what has happened in your life? What do you need to do to take more responsibility for your life?

- **Commitment:** What are you committed to in your life? Are you making a wholehearted commitment?

Step 10:
Be Authentic

You Are Enough

To thine own self be true.

—William Shakespeare

Reflect on these statements and notice your reaction.

"You can say or do something stupid and be incredibly smart."

"You can fail at your job and be very talented."

"You can divorce and be a wonderful partner."

Do these statements resonate with you, or do you feel resistance? The take away from these ideas is that we can be imperfect—even experience failure—and still retain our intrinsic value, our worthiness. What happens to us is not the story of who we are. We are changed by it; we evolve from it; we develop new relationships to ourselves and others because of it; but the experience is not who we are. Divorce does not define you or reflect your ability to be a terrific partner with the right person.

Your readiness to accept imperfection correlates with your readiness to live authentically. Ask yourself: Am I willing to be a work in progress? What will it take for you to say yes? Embracing imperfection is a significant component of authenticity. At the core of authenticity is a belief in your own worthiness. And believing in your own worthiness includes accepting your flaws and quirks and putting yourself out there, confident in your value. You are a work in progress and proud of it. When you embrace this, you are freed from hiding parts of yourself or experiences that you fear are less than desirable.

Dr. Brené Brown, an expert on authenticity and vulnerability, sums it up in her book, *The Gifts of Imperfection*: "When we spend a lifetime trying to distance ourselves from the parts of our lives that don't fit in with who we think we're supposed to be, we stand outside of our stories and hustle for our worthiness by constantly performing, perfecting, pleasing and providing."

Nothing is more empowering than believing you are enough. Knowing this truth at a core level gives you strength and peace. And peace is what is so valuable following the tumult of a divorce. If during your marriage you felt "less than" or allowed your spouse to frame you in a negative light, you need to get real with who you are.

Being authentic means living in alignment with who you are. It is your internal compass pointing true north each time you make a choice that is in congruence with your values. It is being truly attuned to who you are. It means showing up consistently in spite of external pressures, varying social settings, or differing life circumstances. Authenticity emphasizes one's relationship to his or her situation and not the situation itself. The focus is on what you are bringing to *it* instead of what the *it* is. You are empowered because you aren't concerned with other people's reactions. Instead, your focus is: How does my response to this person or situation reflect my core values? Is the choice I am making living in integrity with who I am?

Brown defines authenticity as a "collection of choices that we have to make every day. It's about the choice to show up and be real. The choice to be honest. The choice to let our true selves be seen."

Think of the small choices you make each day. You are at work and there is social gathering that your boss wants you to go to. It will give you visibility with the right people. Attending means you have to rearrange a dinner you have scheduled with a friend. You decide that this is a friend who you see all the time, so they'll understand and you attend the work gathering. You've checked in with yourself and this is not outside your value system.

The following week, you are out of town on a business trip and a couple of your coworkers, one of whom is your manager, want to go to a strip club. This makes you feel uncomfortable and is outside of your personal values. What do you choose? Do you go anyway? Do you make an excuse about why you can't, or do you come out and say, "That isn't my scene. See you in the morning."

Living authentically isn't about making the right choice; it is about making your choice—the choice that is in alignment with who you are. You want to be aware of your boundaries and ask: What am I willing or unwilling to do to make my working or personal relationships work that doesn't compromise who I am?

The expression "she seems comfortable in her own skin" is an instinctive reaction people experience when engaging with an authentic individual. Sometimes you can't put your finger on it, but you know authenticity when you experience it. In the presence of an authentic person, you feel at ease and unguarded. Such people invite trust and create a feeling of comfort in those around them because you intuitively know you are safe. You may not even like or agree with the person, but you trust them because they are revealing who they truly are. You sense that what you see is what you get in public and in private. Such people instinctively draw others.

Contrast this to reactions you may experience when in the presence of an inauthentic individual. You've seen them; they are chameleons. After a conversation with such a person, you may find yourself wondering why you can't seem to gain traction. There doesn't seem to be anything to grasp onto in the relationship. Instinctively you assume a guarded posture or feel a vague sense of unease and wariness. You sense that what they are presenting to you in this moment may look very different from what they present in a different setting or in private. Who are they?

Authentic people don't have to cover up parts they believe undesirable to others because they accept their whole selves. When you don't feel you have to hide parts of yourself, you can relax and avoid the stress that accompanies the fear of being found out. When you're connected to your core values, you know how you need to move through the world and with whom you want to interact. There are some key benefits.

- More confidence: Each time you assert yourself in the world, your self-image becomes stronger.

- Less stress: You aren't concerned about fitting in.

- Personal empowerment: You control how you respond to people and situations. Your emotions don't rule you.

- Self-connection: You move with intention because you know what is important to you.

- Connection to others: You reveal who you are and attract those of like spirit.

- Freedom: You aren't shackled to masks and roles to please others.

These are some really compelling benefits, so why is it so difficult to remove the mask?

Consider your marriage. How did you experience who you were within your relationship? You may have played a role in an effort to make the relationship work. You may have tried to reveal yourself early on, only to be met with criticism. You were "too emotional," "too irrational," or too whatever. Maybe you made a mistake and were judged very harshly. Your brain filed the message that you weren't enough. You may have then started to hide the part of yourself that met with disapproval in an effort to be more like the person your spouse wanted. If you were more perfect, your partner would behave differently or love you more.

These beliefs cause people to put on masks. See if any resonate with you.

- You suspect you aren't enough. You believe there are unlikable parts of you and you would be abandoned (again) if anyone knew about them.

- You were vulnerable in your marriage, and you got burned. Why open yourself again?

- Hiding yourself feels safe. If someone doesn't really know you, they can't dislike you.

- There was the lunch table in high school where the

cool kids sat and you still want a seat at that table. You'll never get one if they really know you.

- You suspect others will think less of you because you are divorced. They will think something must be wrong with you.

What fear is common to all these beliefs? The fear of rejection is so palpably painful, we will don any mask to avoid it. However, if no one really knows us, we have walled ourselves off from the possibility of having real relationships—with ourselves and with others. That decision has many costs.

- Disconnection from yourself: You get lost in your role(s).

- Inability to be loved: You can't ever be truly loved and accepted if you don't allow people to see the real you.

- Loss of personal power: You are ruled by your fears and insecurities.

- Depleted energy: Your energy is being used to assume a role, leaving you an inadequate amount to pursue a fulfilling, happy life

A Story from Julie

My clients, Pete and Mary, were in their seventies and had been married for 16 years. This was the second marriage for both. Even after 16 years, they still carried the shame from being divorced. Each had children with his or her first spouse. The couple moved to a new town and introduced the adult children as their biological children to anyone they met. They instructed the kids to call them Mom or Dad in public, though the step-kids used first names in private. The adult children were further instructed not to make any mention of the parents' prior marriages. When one daughter asked why, she was informed that no one in town knew that Pete and Mary had been divorced and they wanted to keep it that way.

How can you begin to drop your mask? Start with just becoming more aware. Be attuned to situations that trigger the donning of the mask. Who are you with? What is the setting? What is really at stake in this situation for you? When you increase your awareness, you can begin to challenge the messages or beliefs you hold. For example, will you literally die if someone rejects you or doesn't like you? What is the worst that can happen? What if you simply chose to believe that if, once you have shared, that person doesn't like you, they weren't the one to appreciate what you offer—but someone else will?

Yes, when you reveal yourself to others, you will be subject to potential judgment, criticism, and even rejection. The amount of power you grant your fears is within your control. Try turning the tables on how you view vulnerability. Instead of seeing it as a potential path to being hurt (again), what if you viewed it in an expansive light? When you reveal yourself, you are opening yourself to new opportunities.

Consider how revealing yourself is an expression of power. In putting yourself out there, you are tacitly declaring you believe you are worthy. You are confident that you can handle what life presents—the possibility of being hurt does not send you cowering. In revealing yourself, you are claiming the reward of a fulfilling relationship in which who you are honored, appreciated, and valued. And you aren't allowing your fear of rejection to occupy a position of power over you.

Divorce, even in the most civilized of cases, is an emotionaly bruising process, but it doesn't need to leave permanent scars. Embracing the cuts and scrapes along the way rather than creating an impenetrable wall will ultimately help you heal. Being self-aware, you can accept your limitations as well as your strengths. You have a keen awareness that perfection doesn't exist; flaws are inevitable and sometimes you won't show up as well as you'd like. But key to authenticity is acceptance: You are OK with who you are.

And if you aren't sure who that is any longer, reflect upon how you reveal yourself when you are among friends and family. Are you sharing your beliefs, values, and ideas? In the end, you want the acceptance of the people who really know you for all that you are. You may not have the most friends, but you'll have the best ones because they will be the ones who really know you and value what you have to offer.

Exercise

In your journal, write your answers to the following questions.

- Reflect upon the mask(s) you wear. What do they look like?

- In which situations or from whom do you want to hide?

- Which fears within you are being triggered? Write them down. Acknowledge them.

- Now ask yourself how much control do you want to grant these fears? How can they just occupy some space without taking over?

- What could you do if you didn't operate from a place of fear? Who could you be?

- What would it take for you to drop the mask? What kind of support do you need?

You are enough

You are the sky. Everything else—it's just the weather.
—PEMA CHÖDRÖN

At the core, we are all equal. Nobody is more worthy than anybody else. This is the truth. Only when you realize that you are already perfect at your core are you able to shine with one hundred percent authenticity.

Theodore Roosevelt said, "Comparison is the thief of joy." Buddhists say that a shortcut to suffering is comparing yourself to other people. Why would you want to be anyone else? When we compare ourselves to others it is a sure way to come up short because it is not possible to be someone else.

While you are trying to be as somebody else, or fit in with a certain group, you miss out on being the real you. You can only be the best you, you know how to be.

Am I Good Enough?

Most of us grew up believing that something is wrong with us. Over time we can work to undo this conditioning; however, overcoming it takes practice and persistence.

As you navigate your process in healing from divorce, pain will inevitably show up. Often we take this personally. We think this is because we are somehow deficient. Maybe we think we are weak or a victim. When things seem wrong, the source of the wrong becomes you.

Even if your parents were well-meaning, they gave messages about how to be special, look a certain way, win, succeed, make a difference, and not be too loud or too shy or too demanding—or especially too needy. To be needy is to be shamed. We value strength, independence, and self-reliance in our culture. To be anything else is to be in contempt.

The real truth is that we all have needs. Being told that our natural way of being is not right says that somehow we are unworthy.

Anxiety and Unworthiness

Most of our suffering in the process of divorce and other deep transitions in our life centers on anxiety. This anxiety stems from trying to protect ourselves from a core negative belief about who we are.

Not wanting to feel bad about ourselves, we create what are called deficiency motivations. For example, if we think we are not smart enough, we try to act smart. We show off how many books we have read or try to sound smart in other ways. If we think we are not pretty enough, we might constantly compare ourselves to others. If we think we are not masculine enough, then we might try risky sports or adventures or be contemptuous of anything weak or feminine.

All of these defensive stances are just a way to stop feeling anxiety about the fear that we are not lovable or good enough. We think that if anyone really knew how deficient we really are, they wouldn't love us.

When you realize that you are good enough, you choose to take refuge in the ground of your own true nature and set yourself free.

Charting True North

Do not anticipate trouble, or worry about what may never happen. Keep in the sunlight.
—Benjamin Franklin

What does "keep in the sunlight" mean to you? It can mean that you don't allow yourself to become overshadowed by someone else. Step out of their story and into the light of your own. Whatever it means to you, it is powerful advice. If you will keep in the light, what a rewarding life you will have. What peace— even happiness—you will experience. Let these words become your call to action.

Choose Optimism with Intention

Choosing to keep in the light isn't passive. You make these choices every day, but may not be aware of them. For example, two friends may call you. One of them always makes you laugh and the other is constantly embroiled in some drama. Who do you choose to call back?

Reflect on a challenge at work. Do you throw up your hands in despair and feel helpless, or do you try to find different means to influence or resolve the situation?

Finally, what do you tell yourself about your divorce? Do you feel it is your fault? Do you think you will feel lousy forever, and it is the worst thing in the world that could ever befall you? Or do you consider it a huge personal challenge that is a temporary setback from which you will rebound and find other possibilities for happiness?

The choices you make run the gamut from who to hang out with to how you rebound from huge life transitions. But each day to varying degrees, you are making choices in accordance with an optimistic or a pessimistic outlook. The key is to be intentional about how you decide and choose in alignment with a determination to keep in the light. This will guide you to seek healthy relationships and rewarding employment. It will support the belief that it is within your power to create a good life. Optimistic people see possibilities and expect success.

A Story from Julie

It was a gravitational pull toward light that made me decide to divorce my husband. I was still married when my dad sent me a box of childhood photos from when I was a baby through my early teens. As I looked through them, I realized I was smiling broadly in every picture. And not a fake, "say cheese" smile, but a wide, teeth-bared, eye-crinkling smile that just bespoke joy and genuine pleasure. My feelings were palpable. Being happy was my true nature. Being optimistic was my true nature. I contrasted this with the state of fatigue that managing a difficult marriage and living with a mercurial husband had caused. Instead of feeling buoyant and hopeful, I felt bogged down and weary. Standing there with the box of photos, it hit me how far I had drifted from that smiling girl. I had allowed someone else to eclipse my sun. I didn't laugh as often as I used to, and I wanted to laugh again. That smiling girl was inside me, and I needed to choose to be her again.

How can you choose to reunite with your smile? It's tough to look for the good during days, weeks, and months when none seems evident. There are always opportunities to dwell on the half empty glass, particularly following a divorce. But if you can look for even a speck of brightness and move toward it, you will heal. You will ultimately thrive as the speck grows in size and becomes your North Star, beckoning you to better things.

Learn to Be Optimistic

In Dr. Martin Seligman's groundbreaking book, *Learned Optimism*, he explains optimism in terms of how people explain their own successes or failures to themselves. How do you explain adversity to yourself? What is your reaction? He posits that people who are optimistic see a failure as due to something external to them that can be changed so that they can succeed next time around. Pessimists tend to view bad events as their fault, lasting a long time, and pervasive. The good news here is that optimism, like resilience and focus, can be learned. If you are pessimistic today, you don't need to be forever. Seligman calls challenging negative beliefs you have in reaction to adversity as "de-catastrophizing."

Psychologists use the term self-efficacy to describe the belief that one has mastery over the events of one's life and can meet challenges as they arise. Albert Bandura, a psychologist, sums it up: "People who have a sense of self-efficacy bounce back from failures; they approach things in terms of how to handle them rather than worrying about what can go wrong."

Looking at this belief in context of Benjamin Franklin's words at the beginning of this chapter, it is clear Franklin was describing self-efficacy. If you believe you can master your life and handle the obstacles and failures that will happen from time to time, there is no need to worry about the future. You feel empowered to handle whatever arises, and you believe you will have some control over the outcome.

So how can you take mastery of your life right now? Here are some suggestions.

Seek Optimistic People

Surround yourself with people who are light—not in the sense of flaky and shallow—but people who look for and see the good. Embrace people who don't dwell in drama. These are the friends who are supportive and genuinely want you to be happy. You have encountered the other type—the complainers who live in a storm cloud. They like the victim role, or at least they refuse to budge from it.

Act As If

In Step 6, we talked about the concept of acting as if: not waiting to feel like doing something before you do it. Keeping positive is an example of this. You may feel so down. You feel like a fraud responding to people that you are doing well, or at least better than you were. Eventually if you say it enough, you do start to believe it and your brain will get the message and follow. Optimism is a motivator.

Look for the Good

Take it day by day. Each day (including the darkest) presents something that, if it isn't good, at least isn't bad. During down times when you don't feel grateful for anything, reflect on the peaceful moments in the day. There might be an hour, or a half hour, during which the anxiety lifted. These moments are gifts. If you can feel that for five minutes, you know you can feel it for increasingly longer periods of times and that engenders hope.

Check Your Story

When mourning your marriage, reflect on how often you smiled versus cried or felt anxious during your relationship. Whether it was your choice or your spouse's, in the aftermath of a divorce, few people can say their marriage was really happy and they were happy in it. It might have been in the beginning, but by the time it ended, you had had your share of unhappiness and concerns. Now that it is over, you have an opportunity to smile again. You are your own joy potential. It is up to you to stay in the sunlight. You may not feel like smiling now, but try to remember things that made you smile when you weren't embroiled in your divorce. How can you reconnect with them? How can you reconnect with your own true nature?

Exercise

Each day, consider what is working in your favor. It may simply be that you are alive, or you have a place to live, or that it was sunny that day. You can say the same thing each day if that is what is true for you. Eventually you will be able to add to the list. For now, it is just important to get a list and be intentional about what in your life is positive.

- What makes you smile?

- When was the last time you felt joy?

- How about the last time you really had a belly laugh? What was going on? Who was there?

- What is one small thing you can do to get closer to your joy?

- Think about people, activities, pets, hobbies, or anything else that makes you feel lighter when you think about them. Create a list.

- What do you tell yourself about your divorce? How do you interpret the challenge?

- Is there a way you can de-castastrophize some of your beliefs? What are indisputable facts and how long will these be true? What are some beliefs that may not be factual? How could you move forward if you disputed these?

A Letter to You from Julie

....

As you finish this book, where are you? Are you hopeful and excited about the future? Are you struggling to make it through the day? Are you somewhere in the space between? If you feel like you are barely hanging on, take a moment to celebrate that you are hanging on. It's tough and you don't have to hang on gracefully—just keep hanging on. Eventually your grip will evolve into an embrace, an embrace of the good things you will attract to your life.

Adrenaline sees you through the divorce, with euphoria quickly following as the immediate unpleasantness ends. But then there is a big empty space to fill. There is a feeling of let down as the adrenaline dissipates and the euphoria wanes. The sudden discovery of space feels like emptiness. Even if it is filled with work, to-do lists, and childcare, it is different. At times it may feel exciting and at other times daunting.

What can you create to fill the space that will matter?

Once the divorce is over, your friends are checking it off the list. OK, time to move on, that's done! They're not going to ask you every day how you're doing. You're supposed to be moving on! They've seen you through your crisis.

It's funny, but don't you feel there is an unspoken understanding about the amount of time you are allowed to grieve before you are viewed as moribund? Tacitly your friends are shouting, "Excelsior!"

What are you supposed to do to move on? What does that look like? Is moving on being able to get out of bed and go to work? Is it dating? Is it moving or starting a new career you've always dreamed of?

From the outside I may not appear as if I have moved on. My court date has come and gone, but I don't feel ready to date. I have moments of sadness. I still feel disappointment. From time to time I find myself looking at my friends' happy marriages and wondering how I didn't choose better. Why couldn't that be me? At times loneliness creeps in when planning a weekend or vacation. My friends are all married, many with kids, and they are not free to just up and go. It feels like a couples' world.

But there are times I revel in the freedom. There is no one to judge how I spend time or criticize the way I live. I can make plans to get together with whomever, whenever. I can cook the way I want to cook—by dragging every utensil and ingredient from the kitchen cabinets and creating a big chaotic heap on the counter. I can choose to travel more for my work. I can watch the preshow for the Oscars on E! and read any silly magazine I choose.

Are any of these things better than a meaningful, caring relationship? No, but it's what I celebrate now because after years of trying to make something work, this stuff seems good. I feel at peace. And I've learned that enjoying the small happy stuff is at the root of getting ready for the bigger happy stuff that I believe is in the future. And I do believe the future is bright.

Each day I try to reflect on what I am grateful for, big and small. I am so grateful for my friends and family. And I am forever grateful to each repairperson and handyman who showed up on time to the house the first winter that I was alone. They didn't overcharge and displayed patient kindness toward a newly single woman who had no clue about ice dams or winterizing lawn mowers. And I sure am grateful to a friend who told me to hire someone to plow the driveway during one of the snowiest winters on record in the Northeast.

So what are the takeaways from the misery that is divorce? You'll have your own. Write them down. It helps to see that you learned something and didn't just suffer. Here are mine.

- Serenity is amazingly good. Striving for serenity seems more important than seeking happiness.

- I need to meet people where they are and not where I wish they were.

- When someone shows me who they are, I need to believe them instead of hanging on to an unfounded belief in his or her untapped potential. It could remain forever untapped.

- Sometimes the devil you know is just that, a devil.

- Behavior and only behavior is what matters.

- I am a fixer and need to cut it out.

- There is no script for life, and the people who are most successful can ad lib really well.

- I can survive disappointment and heartache; I am resilient.

I don't know what lies ahead. You probably don't either. Having gone through divorce and experienced gut-wrenching sorrow, I feel more at peace with the unknown. There will be challenges to face and other disappointments, but I think a gift of divorce is that you and I have had our mettle tested. We have walked through fire and survived, and that is powerful. After all, if you can survive divorce, don't you feel you can handle pretty much anything? That lifts the burden of worrying about the future.

I have learned the thing that matters most is how well you feel you are showing up to your life, and if that means you don't get what you had hoped for, you can choose another vision, another dream.

Another gift is that you and I know who we can count on. I know the friends who were there when the chips were down and now they are closer. And the ones who weren't? Well, you had to find out sometime.

Good will come and you will be there to receive it, to embrace it. This is what I believe for me and for you.

Wishing you peace and fulfillment,

JULIE

A Letter to You from Judy

And we are put on this earth, a little space that we might learn to bear the beams of love.

—WILLIAM BLAKE

I AM SO GLAD YOU CHOSE TO TAKE THIS PATH WITH US. As you finish this book, may your aspiration for leading a beautiful life become strong. May your compassion for yourself and others increase. When you begin to doubt yourself remember that as your shame decreases, your heart will lighten and you will experience more and more of your fundamental wisdom.

Lead with your heart. That's what it boils down to: Lead with your heart. There is nothing to protect. You have always been safe. You will come to recognize this, to know this deeply. When you relax and trust wholeheartedly in who you are, in the ground of your being, you will stay vital and in love with life regardless of the hardships you encounter.

Say what you feel right now, love what you love right now, in this moment. In order to cross the threshold into a new life, you must let go. You must let go of your ego, your blame, your bitter stories, and recriminations. You must lead with your heart. Love what you love. Put down these things that don't matter, these things that hold you back—that keep the door of your heart shut. The people and the situations that have harmed you are the least important things about you.

Letting go of our stories, blame, and grief is a hard lesson, but it will serve you all of your life. Letting go is the ultimate lesson.

I remember a sunny but cold day in Plymouth, Massachusetts. I was living with my ex-husband in a condo overlooking a golf course in the Pinehills. I took my little dog, a small Chihuahua, Bella, to the market with me. She was a sweet dog, the Velcro kind, loving and affectionate. She couldn't walk very far because of two knee surgeries and a weakened heart. She trusted me completely. We finished our shopping and went back to the condo. I picked up a big bag of groceries, some bottled water, and Bella from the car.

Balancing it all, I walked up the ramp and through the first door into the building. At the second interior door, I hesitated. Perhaps I should set things down and then walk through? No, I just pushed on through, bending over to find the handle of the door, balancing groceries, dog, and all. Then it happened. I dropped Bella. She landed on her stomach on the concrete floor, legs splayed. I dropped to my knees. She couldn't get her breath. I could see her struggling, her little weakened heart racing. She was frightened and panting. We sat there for a long while, me and Bella, with the groceries on the cold concrete floor. Finally she recovered her breath and I was able to pick her up and hold her. She licked my face. I felt such horror at what I had done. I thought I could push through the door, taking all everything with me. I was stubborn and aggressive—even stressing my beloved little dog. I did not want to waste time, slow down, or let the rules of life apply to me.

It's simple really. My ego blocked me from the reality of my situation. I was given the opportunity to put down my burden, my ego, open the door, cross gently, and pick up what I needed. Time and time again, we are offered the chance to truly learn this: We cannot hold on to things and move forward. You must let go of the things that do not serve you, and life itself. In order to enter your new life, you must let go. Let go of your blame, ego, righteousness, hurt, and all the things that diminish you.

To cross the threshold to a new life, take what is necessary and let go of the rest.

I wish you the very best. I hope that this book has helped you in your journey. I would love to hear from you and even better meet you in person.

It seems appropriate to close with the same powerful quote we opened with:

> *"To journey without being changed is to be a nomad. To change without journeying is to be a chameleon. To journey and to be transformed by the journey is to be a pilgrim."*

We are pilgrims, you and I.

My deepest blessings to you,

JUDY

Judy's Acknowledgements

The idea for this book came to me while going through a painful loss. It is through this loss that I became stronger and happier. The saving grace for me through the ten thousand joys and the ten thousand sorrows of life has been in the truth and wisdom of the dharma. Having studied Buddhism for over 20 years, the wisdom, understanding and support I have been given is immeasurable. My family, Stacie, Shelli, Katie, Winston and Grace are constant reminders to me of how lucky I am to be loved and how much I love them. My cousin Glenda Goehrs has been loving, more than supportive and an advocate of this book. My beloved dharma buddy, June Kramer has been kind, steady and a continuing source of wisdom in my life. Thanks to Ric Winstead who is always, always unconditionally there. Thanks to the test readers for your wonderful help and advice. Deep gratitude to Jane Freidman for her expertise. The deepest thanks to my clients for telling me your stories and allowing me to share your journey.

Thanks to the best pilgrim I have ever known, my grandmother, Gracie Kerley.

Julie's Acknowledgements

With deepest gratitude to: Our intrepid project manager and talented content editor, Jane Friedman, copy editor Melissa Wuske, production designer, Sophia Wiedeman, graphic designer, James Egan of Bookfly Design, and to all our test readers who were so generous with their time and valuable input. We couldn't have written the book without your contributions and support.

I am especially appreciative for all my close friends and colleagues in Seattle and Connecticut who have been incredibly supportive and encouraging through the years in good times and in bad.

My love and special thanks go to my mother and grandmother who raised me to be a strong woman and who are constant sources of inspiration.

ABOUT THE AUTHORS

DR JUDY KENNEDY has been a psychologist for over 20 years. She has helped individuals and couples find meaning in their lives as well as learn and develop effective tools as they deal with transition and other life difficulties. She also works with leaders and executive teams to create not only good business practices but also to create environments of authenticity, meaning and collaboration.

She welcomes your questions and thoughts. Contact her at www.drjudykennedy.com or www.intoabeautifullife.com

JULIE CONNOLLY is a certified executive and personal coach by the International Coach Federation. She founded her company, LifeRecrafted, LLC to specifically address the needs of individuals navigating divorce and other challenging life and career transitions. She does personal coaching in addition to leading workshops focused on divorce recovery, personal power, transition, and effective communication.

Julie has a B.A. in English from Middlebury College, and received her formal coach training at Coach U. However, it is the real life training she received while navigating her own divorce, along with several major career transitions, and physical moves across the country over the past twenty years that inform her coaching and writing.

You can learn more about Julie at www.liferecrafted.com or by visiting her blog http://liferecrafted.com/about-transitions. She welcomes your comments and questions.